GOING ONLINE

In *Going Online*, one of our most respected online learning leaders offers insights into virtual education—what it is, how it works, where it came from, and where it may be headed. Robert Ubell reaches back to the days when distance learning was practiced by mail in correspondence schools, and then leads us on a tour behind the screen, touching on a wide array of topics along the way, including what it takes to teach online and the virtual student experience. You'll learn about:

- how to build a sustainable online program;
- how to create an active learning online course;
- why so many faculty resist teaching online;
- how virtual teamwork enhances digital instruction;
- how to manage online course ownership;
- how learning analytics improves online instruction.

Ubell says that it is not technology alone, but rather unconventional pedagogies, supported by technological innovations, that truly activate today's classrooms. He argues that innovations introduced online—principally peer-to-peer and collaborative learning—offer significantly increased creative learning options across all age groups and educational sectors. This impressive collection, drawn from Ubell's decades of experience as a digital education pioneer, presents a powerful case for embracing online learning for its transformational potential.

Robert Ubell is Vice Dean, Online Learning, at NYU Tandon School of Engineering, where he heads the school's digital education unit. Recipient of the highest honor given for individual achievement in digital education, the A. Frank Mayadas Leadership Award, he is a Fellow of the Online Learning Consortium.

GOING ONLINE

Perspectives on Digital Learning

Robert Ubell

*With a chapter on Active Learning
by John Vivolo*

Routledge
Taylor & Francis Group

NEW YORK AND LONDON

First published 2017
by Routledge
711 Third Avenue, New York, NY 10017

and by Routledge
2 Park Square, Milton Park, Abingdon, Oxon OX14 4RN

Routledge is an imprint of the Taylor & Francis Group, an informa business

© 2017 Taylor & Francis

Library of Congress Cataloging in Publication Data
Names: Ubell, Robert (Vice dean of online learning), author.
Title: Going online : perspectives on digital learning / Robert Ubell.
Description: New York : Routledge, 2017.
Identifiers: LCCN 2016029581| ISBN 9781138025318 (hardback) | ISBN 9781138025325 (pbk.) | ISBN 9781315775173 (ebook)
Subjects: LCSH: Computer-assisted instruction. | Web-based instruction.
Classification: LCC LB1028.5 .U28 2017 | DDC 371.33/4—dc23
LC record available at https://lccn.loc.gov/2016029581

ISBN: 978-1-138-02531-8 (hbk)
ISBN: 978-1-138-02532-5 (pbk)
ISBN: 978-1-315-77517-3 (ebk)

Typeset in Bembo and Stone Sans
by Florence Production Ltd, Stoodleigh, Devon, UK

For Ella, Ben, and Fordon

CONTENTS

FOREWORD

Online education, or digital education, had a strong presence at the NYU Tandon School of Engineering well before it became a topic of conversation in the rest of NYU and much of the academic world. The number of students opting for an occasional online course has been growing steadily in the school, as is the list of Master's programs offered entirely online. Much of this has been happening under the leadership of Robert Ubell, the author of this book, whose firsthand experience with online learning makes him an authority on most aspects of the subject. Not surprisingly, a reader wishing to learn the landscape of online education will find much of value in the book, based on the author's personal perspective over a long period of time, and I am accordingly pleased to recommend it to all those interested in the subject, and more broadly, in the evolution of higher education itself.

Some years ago, more than a few universities saw online learning as the panacea for providing affordable education, and began to invest in the enterprise. But the premise seems to have gone astray for a number of reasons, one or two of which I will discuss momentarily. In spite of much anticipation, online education still lags behind the methodology of conventional education, especially in well-known universities that seem to have a higher stake in the *status quo*. The most successful enterprises that have made tangible inroads are a few MOOCs (Massive Open Online Courses), in existence for some time now, despite some false starts on their part and misgivings on the part of others. It is no surprise that most MOOCs are only loosely tied to universities, at least for now, in part because they decouple education (in broad terms) from the degree-granting privilege. Universities, on the other hand, have successfully worked to keep intact the link between the two, thus preserving their monopoly on education methods as much as on granting degrees.

When I say universities sustain their monopoly, whom do I have in mind? The administrators—at least in those universities without the cushion of rich endowments—are willing to experiment with online education, though most of them don't seem to know how best to do it. Their governing boards are keen as well, having become aware that higher education has become more expensive than can be borne comfortably by a large segment of society, and somehow finding solace in the thought that online education offers a miracle alternative to the sapping costs of higher education. Despite all this willingness, a worry has been that potential employers of graduating students may not regard online education to be on par with the conventional one. However, several potential employers, especially in quantitative subjects, seem to regard as important the proficiency in a subject over the emptiness of the students' pedigree, so one imagines that this change in outlook would nudge the acceptance of online education by parents and students alike. Further, the convenience of online learning for non-traditional students is rather obvious. It is the modern-day alternative to the standard paradigm of a 18-year old fresh out of high school coming in to live with other similarly untested youngsters, and emerging after four years, at considerable expense to themselves and to their parents, with a degree certificate of indifferent value in the modern workforce that demands new and different skills each year. Why, then, has online learning not caught on as much as one may have thought possible? Why is the growth of online learning only linear and incremental, instead of exploding?

If administrators, students, parents and employers are turning favorable, or at least reluctantly, who exactly is holding out? The author assigns a good part of the responsibility to the professoriate. There are good reasons for it and the resistance to change is real and palpable. As a long-time professor myself, one who routinely prided on the quality of his teaching, I feel that I should elaborate this aspect a bit here—in part because, professors have to realize that, with or without their buy-in, things *will* change; the more openly the changes are welcomed, the more orderly will be the evolution of teaching and learning. The change is accelerated by the fact that the so-called contract and adjunct faculty members (i.e., those who teach without tenure or on the tenure-track), whose influence has been increasing significantly in university governance, are more flexible and open to experimentation. Who knows where the system of higher education will go in this century, and what alternative business models the universities will adopt, with pressures felt on several fronts!

Some of the resistance of the professoriate is entrenched culture and the earnest belief that classroom teaching is superior: stated in simplistic terms, it allows eye contact with students and provides the instructor the feedback that is much needed to do his or her job right. One of my Uzbek acquaintances once told me how, when he was teaching in a women's college in a certain country in which women are not allowed to mix with men outside their family, his students had to listen to his lectures from behind an opaque curtain. This was quite disconcerting to him, he said, because he had no idea whether the students were listening to him, playing games with each other, or simply absent. It is no surprise that online education, which invokes similar scenarios, is thought to be not only an impersonal substitute but "an interloper with little to recommend it." I suspect that the professors are also unwilling to give up the emotional gratification that they receive after delivering a lecture well, and the instant satisfaction from the knowledge that the students understood what was said, a kind of high that sustains good mood for the entire day.

Online learning has moved well past the stage where interaction with students is absent, and it no longer helps to be haunted by memories of their primitive technological state of yesteryears. Technology has evolved and the nature of interactions between students and the professor has changed so much that one can decide what is most important to the professor and the students and adapt the online lectures to approximate those needs. Here, the lapse is at least in part one of communication, and university administrators and professors have not done a good job of integrating their respective thinking with technology people. The student body itself has evolved—and gone are the days when they sat listening to the professor attentively and with starry-eyes: the myriad distractions that modern smart phones bring with them have changed classroom participation. The students sometimes better absorb content via technology rather than via lectures delivered in person.

As the technology has changed and the modes of online delivery have evolved, professors have to relearn the art of teaching: it no longer suffices to walk into a classroom with the firm conviction that what worked for them as students will work for theirs now. This redefinition takes some extra time and effort on the part of the professor but the rewards of gratification should be as great or greater. This is the point that needs to be emphasized until the online mode of lecture delivery becomes as well accepted as the classroom delivery. Indeed, this is the key ingredient in making a successful transition, since many teachers are driven by a sense of satisfaction that in-person teaching provides.

There are other important issues as well. Quite often, on-campus living teaches college students valuable lessons in becoming useful citizens of the world, and sometimes in upholding idealism in favor of pragmatism; and no one who believes in the value of experiential learning is keen to deny the value of a student cohort. In the long run, even those who love to see online learning become a significant part of university learning scenario do not imagine classrooms to disappear, or universities to turn entirely virtual. In several discussions I have had with the university faculty, I have seen little resistance to the notion that experiential learning—or hands-on learning—is preferred, except for the cautionary and pragmatic note on efficiency and cost. To advocate online education seriously, we have to make the case that it is the right means for experiential learning without diminishing possibilities. Though this point has been made by the author, it could be more pervasive and stronger; but I should not quibble about this otherwise very interesting account of online learning.

K. R. Sreenivasan, President and Dean,
Tandon School of Engineering, New York University

ACKNOWLEDGMENTS

The reflex response to online learning from most people is almost immediately to wonder "Is it any good?". What's curious about this nearly universal question is that the Internet has invaded almost every other part of our lives—without raising that puzzled interrogation. A source of pleasure, recreation, commerce, communication, and knowledge for more than three billion people everywhere, we go online to shop, work, search, gossip, and perform nearly every act that matters in our human repertoire. While nearly every other Internet activity is pursued breathlessly with hardly any argument, virtual education remains a question mark. Even though research tells us that digital instruction is as good as—and often better than—face-to-face learning, what matters most is what people believe. These essays do not answer the question about whether online learning is any good. That inquiry has long been settled. But they do make a case for paying attention to virtual education as an intellectually vigorous force in our culture.

This collection covers a couple of decades of engagement with online learning, first at Stevens Institute of Technology and then at New York University. Most appeared in professional periodicals, either in print or online; others as chapters in books. Two essays—one on faculty resistance to online learning (Chapter 5) and another on the unique features of digital education (Chapter 4)—were written expressly for this collection. Nearly all previously published chapters have been updated with recent references and new material. I am especially grateful to my close colleague, John Vivolo, Director of Online and Virtual Learning at NYU Tandon School of Engineering, who graciously agreed to contribute his insightful essay on active learning (Chapter 3). John's creativity and skill in digital instruction shines through his essay. I am equally grateful to my co-authors who generously permitted our two previously published articles to reappear here. Prof. M. Hosein Fallah, a former Stevens Institute of Technology colleague, was among the first to experiment with online learning. Hosein and I collaborated on Chapter 6. A. Frank Mayadas, a pioneer who established the Sloan Consortium (now the Online Learning Consortium), the driving force in launching online education at US colleges and universities, is the co-author of Chapter 7.

I am grateful to the publishers of articles that appeared previously in these publications:

Chapter 1, "Dewey Goes Online," first appeared in an abbreviated form in *EDUCAUSE Quarterly*, Vol. 32, No. 4, December 22, 2009 and later in *Virtual Teamwork: Mastering the Art and Practice of Online Learning and Corporate Collaboration*, John Wiley & Sons, Inc., 2010, pp. xxxiii–xlii.

Chapter 2, "Virtual Team Learning," combines two essays published in *TD*. The first appeared as "Virtual Team Learning," August 2010, pp. 52–57; the second as "How to Run a Virtual Classroom," October 11, 2011, www.td.org/Publications/Magazines/TD/TD-Archive/2011/10/How-to-Run-a-Virtual-Classroom.

Chapter 4, "What You Can Do Online, But Not on Campus," appears in this volume for the first time. I am indebted to NYU Tandon Prof. Anne-Laure Fayard for calling my attention to her insight into writing as an essential element in online education.

Chapter 6, co-authored with M. Hosein Fallah, "Blind Scores in a Graduate Test," was originally published as "Blind Scores in a Graduate Test: Conventional Compared with Web-based Outcomes," in the *Journal of Asynchronous Learning Networks (JALN)*, Vol. 4, No. 2, December 2000.

Chapter 7, co-authored with A. Frank Mayadas, "Migrating Online," originally appeared as "Online Learning Environments," an entry in *The Encyclopedia of Distributed Learning*, SAGE Publications (2004), pp. 345–356.

Chapter 8, "Who Owns What?" first appeared in *EDUCAUSE Quarterly*, No. 1, 2001, pp. 45–47. I am indebted to David Sternbach for his expertise on intellectual property.

Chapter 9, "The Road Not Taken," was originally published as "The Road Not Taken: The Divergence of Corporate and Academic Web Instruction," *Journal of Asynchronous Learning Networks (JALN)*, Vol. 14, No. 2, November 2010, pp. 3–8.

Chapter 10, "Engineers Turn to Online Learning," was published originally as "Engineers Turn to e-Learning" in *IEEE Spectrum*, Vol. 37, No. 10, October 2000, pp. 59–63.

★   ★   ★

Dean of the NYU Tandon School of Engineering Katepalli R. Sreenivasan has been among the university's most ardent champions of digital education, urging faculty to experiment with new ways of teaching. It has been enormously gratifying to work closely with him, a scholar, noted not only for his commitment to inventive research, but for his deep sense of academic purpose. I owe "Sreeni" my deep appreciation for his generous support and thoughtful guidance. I am equally indebted to Chandrika Tandon, who immediately recognized the crucial value of online learning to the Engineering School and has supported digital education at NYU faithfully ever since. My gratitude also goes to members of the NYU Tandon Online Faculty Oversight Board—Kurt Becker, Barry Blecherman, Peter Carr, Kristen Day, Mark De Lessio, Dennis Dintino, R. Luke DuBois, Paul Horn, Magued Iskander, Iraj Kalkhoran, Ramesh Karri, Nasir Memon, Bud Mishra, Shivendra Panwar, Bharat Rao, Richard Thorsen, Abraham Ulman, Vivek Veeraiah, and Yao Wang. My gratitude to members of the NYU Tandon Enterprise Learning Board who have given me thoughtful guidance— Amy Abel, Janet Denlinger, Michael Goldstein, Steven Goss, Eugene Innocenti, Diane Davis Jones, Curtis Kendrick, Roy Lowrence, Sandra Milano, Stephanie Mitchko, Harvey Stein, and Allan Weisberg. The wider NYU community has reinforced my commitment to virtual education—Andrew Bates, Brianna Bates, Alex Berthoumieux, Enrico Bertini, Adam Brandenburger, Mgavi Brathwaite, Valarie Cabral, Dinorah Cantú-Pedraza, Justin Cappos, Jonathan Chao, Tom Delaney, Othniel Denis, Vasant Dhar, Ben Esner, Anita Farrington, Julia Freire, Guido Gerig, Ari Ginsberg, Zachary Goldman, Fletcher Griffis, Russ Hamberger, Kathleen Hamilton, Oswaldo Hernandez, Stephen Holmes, Jerry Hultin, John Iacono, Jillian James, Yona Jean-Pierre, Nicole Johnson, Vikram Kapila, Sunil Kumar, Anat Lechner, Yong Liu, Sayar Lonial, I-Tai Lu, Ray Lutzky, Elizabeth McAlpin, Peggy McCready, Joan McDowell, Ben Maddox, Nilsa Marin, Brian Miller, Beth Noveck, Erin O'Brien, Diane Padro, Brad Penuel, Loraine Pizzirusso, Jan Plass, Ryan Poynter, Eric Rasmussen, Neil Radar, Ted Rappaport, Mari Rich, Thomas Reddington, David Rosen, Keith Ross, Ilya Rubenov, Stephen Sagner, Matthew Santirocco, Claudio Silva, Shelton Smith, Kristen Sosulski, Fred Strauss, Torsten Suel, Anup Ved, Phil Venables, Stefaan Verhulst, Peter Voltz, and Eitan Zemel.

I am enormously grateful to my colleagues on the staff of NYU Tandon Online—Ralph Alfieri, Sebastien Auguste, John Barbieri, Lisa Bellantuono, Earl Co, Laura Dicht, Jessie Guy-Ryan, Stephanie Jasmin, Marlene Leekang, Andrew Looke, Luke Modzier, Mayra Ortiz, Daniel Parra, Tameka Roberts, Sara Thermer, Jay VanDerwerken, and John Vivolo. My career in online learning would not have been possible without the knowledge and personal commitment from supportive colleagues at the Online Learning Consortium—Andy DiPaolo, Eric Fredericksen, Ralph Gomory, A. Frank Mayadas, Anthony Picciano, Janet Poley, Peter Shea, and Karen Swan.

I am deeply moved by my family's love and affection—to my daughters Jennifer and Elizabeth and my grandchildren Ella, Ben, and Fordon; to Thornton, Steve, Marielle, Matt, Jack, Shane, and Bryn. To my brothers and step-sisters and their families—Seymour, Marsha, Alvin, Estelle, Evelyn, Anne, Estella, and Ernesto.

To my friends Robert Benton, Hal Espo, Ray Fireman, Martha Gever, Conrad Guettler, Rebecca Harringron, James Holmes, Adam Kaplan, Alice Klein, Andrea Marquez, Robert Millner, Roy Moskowitz, Yvonne Rainer, Gerard Roman, Florence Rowe, Judy Rubin, Neil Salzman, Sheila Slater, and Stephen Stanczyk. My warmest appreciation goes to Elaine Cacciarelli, who has guided this volume from its inception to publication with skill, consistency, and patience. It could not have happened without her. Some of the work in this book was supported by generous grants from the Alfred P. Sloan Foundation, IEEE Foundation and McGraw-Hill Education. Grateful appreciation also goes to the highly professional and dedicated staff at Routledge and its vendor – to my editor Alex Masulis, especially and to his colleague Lauren Schuhmacher, and to Tamsyn Hopkins, Naomi Hill, Meredith Murray, and the team at Florence Production.

Rosalyn's love makes everything possible.

—*Robert Ubell*
New York, 2016

PART I
Virtual Classes

1

DEWEY GOES ONLINE

Nearly a century before the Internet entered college and university life with online learning, the American philosopher and progressive education champion John Dewey recognized that traditional classrooms can often stand in the way of creative learning. Troubled by passive students in regimented rows, Dewey worried that docile students, accepting the unquestioned authority of teachers, not only undermined engaged learning, but thwarted democratic practice in the social and political life of the nation. Instead, Dewey called for a "spirit of free communication, of interchange of ideas" (Dewey, 1915, p. 11), encouraging "active, expressive" learning (Dewey, 1915, p. 20).

Taking up ideas suggested by Dewey and others[1], progressive educators in the 1920s proposed that students learn best by performing real-life activities in collaboration with others. Experiential learning—"learning by doing"—coupled with problem solving and critical thinking, they claimed, is the key to dynamic knowledge acquisition. Rather than respect for authority, they called for diversity, believing that students must be recognized for their individual talent, interests, and cultural identity.

Ever since John Dewey proposed learning by doing as the most fruitful way to absorb and create knowledge, progressive educators have been devising ways to encourage students to get up from their schoolroom seats and do things—experiment, experience, think, and reflect—key principles of *experiential learning*, theorized by the noted scholar David A. Kolb (Kolb, 2015). Often called "hands-on" learning, experiential education is an umbrella concept, under which a number of common and innovative practices fall—case methodology, for example, as well as problem-, project-, and inquiry-based leaning. Lately, "active learning" has become one of the most widely accepted terms (see Chapter 3). The key concept is that merely reading books or listening to lectures is a very poor substitute for discovering and experimenting with concepts and things first-hand. At its best, experiential learning, rather than passively listening to lectures, offers students opportunities to take the initiative, to make decisions on their own. Actively engaged, learners are encouraged to pose questions and solve novel problems, bridging the gap between theory and practice.

In a classic example of experiential education, now more than a century old, some engineering schools open their gates, freeing students to work in industry as part of their undergraduate education. Acknowledging the benefits of learning by doing, cooperative education programs have been sending students off campus for years, experiencing part of their undergraduate studies in college classrooms and labs and partly on the factory floor. Commonly known as "co-op" education, initially launched at Lehigh University in 1901—at about the same time that Dewey was encouraging active learning—and now offered at dozens of college and universities, including Northeastern, Cincinnati, Georgia Tech and others, it provides academic credit for structured job experience, frequently alternating school with work in partnership with an employer (Kerka, 1999).

Working professionals who participate in online programs come to virtual classes already practicing real-life problems on the job. Since only a third of enrollments at US colleges and universities study as residential students, most students today work and go to school part-time (NCES, 2016). Many take courses online, participating in an unprecedented national experiment in *informal* co-op education. Unlike their peers in co-op programs, they are not guided by faculty nor do they receive academic credit for their work experience. Pursuing part-time online academic studies in parallel with their jobs, many work in the same or similar fields as in school, absorbing the theory of their disciplines online while they practice at work. Others go online to increase their competencies in domains for which they lack critical skills. Still others gain knowledge in new disciplines in order to leave those they're in. The freedom open to virtual students is vast. Students can go online, taking classes anywhere in the country or around the world to study at schools where their career objectives correspond with the curricula offered by college and universities far from home. Before the introduction of virtual education, workers were forced to quit their jobs and uproot themselves to study at faraway schools. Today, many stay at their jobs, acquiring the knowledge and credentials they need online.

Can experiential learning be done online (Bates, 2014)? The answer is embedded in the very practice of digital education itself. Participating in an online course is a creative form of experiential learning. As a virtual student, you engage in real-world communication practices, employed by workers and scholars everywhere. Using the technologies that drive digital courses—e-mail, chat, video, multimedia, collaborative software, simulations—virtual students exploit the tools used routinely by executives, academics, scientists, and engineers worldwide. Commerce, scholarship, personal relations today are commonly conducted online. By contrast, the classroom, despite its face-to-face medium, is artificial, often a space for listening, rarely open to practice and reflection (see Chapter 4). No other human engagement, except perhaps theater and spectator sports, is as unlike real-life as the classroom, with students fixed in their seats in rows. In the far more real world of virtual instruction, students are liberated from their inert positions in class to participate daily in extended digital conversations as they do with friends, family, peers, and coworkers. Perhaps, the most remarkable thing about digital education is that its very form is experiential, requiring skill to become expert as a virtual student. Just like learning how to play a musical instrument, digital students must acquire essential competencies, absorbing far more proficiency than on-campus students, whose only effort is to walk into the class and take a seat. One example is the virtual lab, now common in computer science, bioinformatics, business analytics, knowledge management, and other advanced fields. Today, digital students can manipulate the same software remotely as do scientists, engineers, and scholars (Waldrop, 2013). Accessing large-scale systems remotely is now possible in many industries, with virtual students performing experiments or running operations remotely with the same facility as those on site. Virtual education emerges as a workshop in which online students exercise functions essential for scholarship and professional life. Following Dewey, digital learning hones contemporary workplace skills—teamwork, problems-solving, reflection.

Building on the work of Dewey and others, constructivist[2] ideas emerged in the 1970s and 1980s. Constructivists believed that knowledge is built on experience mediated by one's own prior knowledge and the experience of others, a philosophical tradition that goes back to Immanuel Kant. According to construc-tivists, learning is a socially adaptive process of assimilation, accommodation, and correction. For constructivists, students generate new knowledge on the foundation of previous learning.

By contrast, objectivists[3] believe that learning results from the passive transmis-sion of information from instructor to student. For them, reception, not construc-tion, is the key. Objectivists assume that reality is entirely open to observation, independent of our minds. Modern neuroscience appears to support the alternative constructivist claim, concluding that the brain is not a recording device, but rather, the mind actively constructs reality, with experience filtered through a cognitive framework of memories, expectations, and emotions (Dehaene, 2002).

Progressive education was never widely embraced. Apart from a handful of elementary and high schools and a few colleges,[4] for the most part over the last century, schools rejected progressive theories, preferring conventional practice instead, with students seated in rows facing the teacher, a scene reminiscent of turn-of-the-century vintage schoolroom photographs. Face-to-face teaching, the most common style of instruction, and consequently, the practice that appears to be most natural, is often valorized as the foundation against which all other methods are measured (Russell, 2001). It is taken for granted that the classroom is the normal place for learning. Yet there is little evidence to support the claim that traditional education is the standard. The basic assumption is that face-to-face students form a cohesive group, participating alike in discussion, listening to lectures, building intellectual and social relationships with teachers and peers inside and outside class (see Chapter 5). But as Anthony Picciano points out, this is not always the case. Classroom students often feel alienated, drawing away from others and isolating themselves (Picciano, 2002). A significant population feels estranged and falls into a pattern of failure.

Conventional education assumes that because students occupy the same space and are subject to the same conditions, they are fairly similar and should emerge with the same or similar learning outcomes, regardless of the economic or social status. Because students are visible at their desks—rather than invisible in a virtual classroom—somehow we assume that we can know them and understand them. We believe that when we see students in physical space, we can actually gain access to them. Yet it's their invisible qualities that mostly determine who they are. According to Pierre Bourdieu, we forget that the truth of any interaction is never captured entirely by observation (Bourdieu, 1989). So, while face-to-face interaction is often thought of as giving us perfect knowledge of student behavior, in fact, physical presence can often obscure crucially hidden social and psychological relations.

We tend to believe that visual cues—facial expressions and body language—offer us sufficient social communication markers to understand one another. Yet these actions, while open to inspection, fail to give us access to unseen psychological and status relationships to which we are often blind. The classroom resists distinctions that are formed by groups and hierarchies that crisscross it from outside. Traditional instruction—especially the classroom lecture—is a one-size-fits-all product that ignores student identities as multiple, overlapping constellations of real and imaginary selves.

What is visible can often be damaging, turning common experience against us (see Chapter 4). Hair style, clothes, our perceived ideas of physical beauty, and other personal characteristics can often undermine us, even as they have the capacity to move us closer together. The classroom is a place where ordinary misperceptions by teachers and students can easily defeat effective learning. It is place where ethnicity, gender, and race are in plain sight, sadly subject to the same stereotypes and prejudices found on the streets. Online, however, students are often able to enter the virtual classroom anonymously, avoiding the stigmatization that can occur in a physical space (Kassop, 2003).

Dewey raised his voice against the ordinary schoolroom, a place made almost exclusively "for listening." Following Dewey, Paulo Freire recognized the narrative character of the teacher-student relationship. "Education is suffering from a narration sickness," Freire observed and famously ridiculed conventional instruction for its "banking concept of education," with students mechanically memorizing content, turning them into instructional depositories (Freire, 1970).

Today, the demands of online learning—finding unprecedented ways to engage invisible students—have reclaimed Dewey. Suddenly, the lessons of progressive education and the constructivist legacy have become relevant. Rather than being discarded, Dewey is now seen as prescient. In one of the principal online learning research texts, Starr Roxanne Hiltz and her colleagues claim that collaborative online learning "is one of the most important implementations of the constructivist approach" (Hiltz & Goldman, 2005).

Constructivist strategies were introduced in online education and in virtual teams in industry to overcome what Karen Sobel Lojeski and Richard Reilly call "virtual distance," a consequence of a number of potentially alienating factors (Lojeski & Reilly, 2008). Members of virtual teams are often widely separated geographically, with many located in distant time zones. Frequently composed of students from different cultures, who work in different organizations, with unfamiliar standards and models of behavior, virtual teams may also consist of participants with varying technical proficiency.

According to Lojeski and Reilly, virtual distance is composed of three principal disturbances—physical, operational, and affinity distance, with physical distance emerging from obvious disparities in space and time. Operational distance, on the other hand, grows out of workplace dysfunction, such as communication failure— for example, receiving an e-mail from a colleague whose poorly articulated text cannot be deciphered. Affinity distance reflects emotional barriers that stand in the way of effective collaboration. Lojeski and Reilly claim that absence of affinity among team members is the greatest obstacle to quality performance. For them, reducing emotional estrangement in groups is the single most important task.

Pedagogy has never played a significant role in higher education. Instructors walk into most college classrooms without any special training in teaching skills. In universities, pedagogy is often dismissed as a discipline appropriate for kinder-garten and elementary school, not a proper subject for higher education. With online learning, however, pedagogy emerges as a necessity. Without training in how to engage students, helping to close the online psychological gap, faculty are essentially unprepared to teach. In a turnaround, faculty now demand that they receive quality instruction about how to teach online before they enter their virtual classroom; otherwise they feel stranded. For many, teaching online often requires wholesale reconsideration and reformulation of subject matter and delivery, an assessment that can lead to rejuvenating faculty engagement and heighten the granularity of content.

Still, teaching online can be quite disorienting. Faculty can no longer rely on their ability to deliver performances that engage students intellectually and emotionally. In classrooms, professors practice many of the techniques employed by stage actors —rehearsal, scripting, improvisation, characterization, and stage presence (Pineau, 1994). Exploiting tension, timing, counterpoint, and humor with dramatic effect, skilled classroom teachers exhibit qualities that can stimulate thought and action. We are often drawn to content and energized by instructional performances.

But a practiced, smooth presentation can also hide the struggles that go into its creation. It can mask dislocations, errors, and false starts out of which lectures—and the multiple, contradictory acts of learning—are actually assembled. In the *Wizard of Oz*, when Toto pulls the curtain aside, the Wizard's booming, confident authority is revealed as merely manipulation by an ordinary man engineering his false self. According to the French theorist Jacques Rancièr, the instructor's expert delivery may create deep fissures between the student and teacher (Rancière, 1991). While both may be physically in the same space in a classroom, faculty and student can be in far different places emotionally. The more skilled the lecture—often fascinating and pleasurable as in a stage perform-ance—the more it may give the illusion that students have actually absorbed the lesson.

Unwittingly, the lecture contrasts the faculty's apparent confidence against the student's feelings of inadequacy. In a lecture, professors leave their uncertainty behind, submerging the battles they fought to generate a coherent narrative—struggles students are yet to face. In class, instructors present what is known at the very moment when students take their first steps into the unknown. Students soon discover that learning is a gradual, often stumbling process that can lead down blind alleys, often hobbled by false starts. Marked by ruptures and dislocations, learning is a risk-taking exercise, not an elegant performance.

Online learning plays a part in a long trend that has unseated everything that was thought to be ineluctable, moving what was always thought to be at the center to the periphery. Copernicus drove the Earth from the center of the universe to play merely a supporting role in a minor galaxy. Darwin displaced men and women as the pinnacle of creation, placing them as accidental creatures in a long evolutionary drama. While not as momentous, online learning, too, overturns conventional wisdom by drawing professors away from the front of the class-room and moving them to the side as observers (Ubell, 2004).

While the authority of the faculty appears diminished in online teaching, their role is now no longer simply as a performer of narrative lessons. Online, they play a new part as complex agents of intellectual transformation. Merely assigning students to groups and encouraging them to work together will not yield results. Students are not automatically transformed into involved and thoughtful partici-pants when they go online. Poorly prepared, peer learning can exacerbate status differences and generate dysfunctional interactions among students (Blumenfeld, 1996). At worst, virtual teaming can result in "the blind leading the blind" or "pooling ignorance" (Topping, 2005). Faculty must orchestrate online learning, building "intellectual scaffolding," prompting students with projects, discussion topics, and questions to encourage them to think deeply, creatively, and interactively (Christudason, 2003). Ironically, moving from physical to online space often calls upon faculty to become far more engaged than in the classroom. Instructors become facilitators, propelling students to engage in discourse through discussion and argument to generate and link ideas.

At their best, online faculty achieve what is known as "teaching presence," a constellation of actions that give students a vivid sense that virtual instructors are fully engaged (Benbunan-Fich, 2005). Teaching presence emerges from online faculty-student interaction and feedback that exploits e-mail, chat, discussion boards, webinars, and other applications that defy the limits of space and time. Unlike the time constraints imposed by the physical classroom, online instructors and students enter a borderless space, open to the possibility of continuous dialog (Kassop, 2003). In asynchronous communication, the give and take of online discussion is conducted at a much slower pace, giving students and teachers time to reflect, with more room for analysis, critique, and problem-solving (Picciano, 2006). Extending online learning to virtual teams, teaching presence recedes as peer-to-peer learning unfolds. Virtual teaming opens online space, allowing students to work together in pursuit of a shared goal or to produce a joint intellectual product. Student-to-student interaction in small groups permits the acquisition of knowledge and skill through collaborative help and support in what is known as "cognitive presence." For virtual teams to succeed, instructors must encourage students to practice collaborative skills—giving and receiving help, sharing and explaining content, and offering feedback, but also interrogation, critique, challenge, argument, and conflict. With the teacher out of sight—whether online or on-campus—student teams are lifted out of their seats and assume positions rarely taken before—as leader, facilitator, reporter, observer, participant (Swann, 2006). Ultimately, online students may achieve what is known as "social presence," a zone in which virtual teammates are not mere mental fictions, but appear seemingly as "real." With virtual teaming, faculty release students from their paternalistic grip, freeing them from pedagogical infantilization, allowing them to find their own way as mature learners. At its best, virtual teaming emancipates students from the hierarchy of conventional education to practice intellectual democracy.

We can trace the history of education over the last decade by mapping the position of teachers as they migrate from the center of the educational stage as principal actors in traditional classrooms, move to the wings in online learning were they assume a supporting role, and finally depart in virtual teams, where they play an entirely new and radical part, setting the stage for students to act all on their own. Faculty now sit in the audience as observers and critics, with students on the platform as performers, occupying an engaged space where learning takes place collaboratively with their peers. Teams disrupt the linear narrative of conventional instruction by introducing overlapping discourse, flowing from multiple sources in discontinuous, mostly asynchronous, peer-to-peer discussion and argument. In the spirit of Dewey, who encouraged learning by doing, the task of teams is to work together to create knowledge. For Dewey, the ideal classroom is a "social clearing-house, where experiences and ideas are exchanged and subjected to criticism, where misconceptions are corrected, and new lines of thought and inquiry are set up" (Dewey, 1915, p. 34). Active learning, he claimed, emerges from students forming a "miniature community, an embryonic society" (Dewey, 1915, p. 13)—uncannily like virtual teams.

Notes

1   Other early leaders of progressive education in the US and abroad were the American educator Francis Parker; German teacher Friedrich Fröbel, who coined the term "kindergarten;" Swiss school reformer Johann Heinrich Pestalozzi; Abraham Flexner, American medical-school reformer; and Johann Friedrich Herbart, German philosopher and psychologist, who first introduced pedagogy as an academic discipline.
2   Chief among constructivist theorists are American cognitive-learning psychologist Jerome Bruner, Swiss developmental psychologist Jean Piaget, and early Soviet psychologist Lev Vigotsky.
3   Principal objectivist theorists were the Russian (and later Soviet) psychologist Ivan Pavlov, famously known for his work on conditioned reflex in salivating dogs, and the American psychologist B. F. Skinner, who championed radical behaviorism in what he called operant conditioning.
4   Among the handful of colleges and universities that continue the progressive education tradition are Bank Street College of Education, Goddard College, Antioch University, and Union Institute and University.

References

Bates, T. (2004) *Can you do experiential learning online? Assessing design models for experiential learning.* Online Learning and Distance Education Resources. Retrieved from: www.tonybates.ca/2014/12/01can-you-do-experiential-learning-online-assessing-design-models-for-experiential-learning/.

Benbunan-Fich, S. R. R. (2005). The online interaction learning model. In R. G. Starr Roxanne Hiltz (Ed.), *Learning together online* (pp. 28–29). Mahwah, NJ: Lawrence Erlbaum.

Blumenfeld, R. M. P (1996). Learning with peers. *Educational Researcher, 25*, 37–39.

Bourdieu, P. (1989). Social space and symbolic power. *Sociological Theory, 7*(1), 14–25.

Christudason, A. (2003). Peer learning. *Successful Learning* (37).

Dehaene, S. (2002). *The cognitive neuroscience of consciousness.* Cambridge, MA: MIT.

Dewey, J. (1915). *The school and society.* Chicago, IL: Chicago University Press.

Freire, P. (1970). *Pedogogy of the oppressed.* New York: Continuum.

Hiltz, S. R., & Goldman, R. (2005). *Learning online together.* Mahwah, NJ: Lawrence Erlbaum.

Kassop, M. (May/June 2003). Ten ways online education matches, or surpasses, face-to-face learning. *The Technology Source Archives, 3*, 1–7.

Kerka, Sandra. (1999) *New Direction for Cooperative Education,* Columbus, OH: Eric Clearinghouse on Adult and Vocational Education.

Lojeski, K. S., & Reilly, R. (2008). *Uniting the virtual workforce.* Hoboken, NJ: John Wiley.

National Center for Educational Statistics. (2016). *The Condition of Education.* Retrieved from: http://nces.ed.gov/programs/coe/indicator_cha.asp.

Picciano, A. (2002). Beyond student peceptions. *JALN, 6*(1), 21–39.

Pineau, E. L. (1994). Teaching is performance. *American Education Journal, 31*(1), 3–25.

Rancière, J. (1991). *The ignorant schoolmaster.* Stanford, CA: Stanford University Press.

Russell, T. (2001). *The no significant difference phenomenon* (5th ed.). Montgomery, AL: IDECC.

Swann, J. S. K. (2006). Assessment and collaboration in online learning. *JALN, 10*(1), 45–62.

Topping, K. (2005). Trends in peer learning. *Educational Psychology, 25*(6), 631–645.

Ubell, F. M. R. (2004). Online learning environments. In K. E. Anna DiStefano (Ed.), *Encyclopedia of distributed learning.* Thousand Oaks, CA: Sage.

This essay first appeared in "Virtual Teamwork," edited by Robert Ubell (Wiley 2010), pp. xxxiii–xlii.

2

VIRTUAL TEAM LEARNING

In Isaac Asimov's robot novel, *The Naked Sun*, people can't stand being in the same room with one another. They hate being face-to-face. In the chilling story that takes place on the futuristic planet of Solaris, where actual personal contact creeps everyone out, Solarians much prefer to be in touch virtually, "viewing" one another on wall-to-wall image panels, much like today's teleprescence screens. While Earthlings are not yet Solarians, in our own sci-fi daily home and work life, we now happily communicate at a distance, even playing Scrabble with strangers on our hand-held devices with delight.

Harnessing the power of virtual worlds is now a necessity, as industry penetrates every corner of our planet and as workers are required to be in touch with teammates in the next block and in far-away continents around the clock. In most companies, participating in virtual teams is no longer an exotic exercise, but a bottom-line requirement. In global companies, technical and managerial staff often set their clocks at sunrise for virtual meetings with members of their across-the-globe teams in Asia, Africa, the Middle East—wherever participants are located. Education and training that exploits virtual teaming not only provides essential collaborative communication skills, but also engages learners in one of the today's most advanced workplace practices. In the new economy, knowing how to interact effectively at 5am in your pajamas with teammates you may never see and whose accents you may find challenging has become a critical competence. Asimov's weird virtual life is no longer a spooky fantasy, but commonplace today. Millions are in constant contact by e-mail, Skype, smartphones, social media, texting, and other remote technologies. At work, interaction is routine by teleconference, webinars, and groupware—and in a handful of places, Second Life and teleprescence. Opportunities to introduce virtual teaming are no longer limited by clunky technical means. You and your workforce now have everything you need on your desktop or in your handheld device to participate in engaged collaboration on the job or in class from anywhere. There are no longer steep barriers to virtual teaming. Following a decade in which corporate training introduced often alienating self-learning modules from which workers dropped out at alarming rates, virtual teaming restores and extends collaboration, giving personnel a chance to interact with each other in engaged, project-based classes. Virtual teaming is a giant step ahead in online learning and a promising leap beyond on-site, instructor-led classrooms. Virtual learning instructor Edward Volchok[1] says that cross-functional teams are essential for a business to deliver superior value to their customers. Teamwork, says Volchok, is the key to engaging other departments to achieve company objectives. According to Volchok, participants in virtual classes learn the art of debating, generating consensus, and delivering cogent proposals under tight deadlines.

Overcoming Virtual Distance

Practiced effectively, virtual teams can overcome what global teamwork experts Karen Sobel Lojeski and Richard Reilly call "virtual distance," a consequence of a number of potentially alienating factors. When your co-workers are invisible, it's not surprisng if you become somewhat disoriented. Often widely separated geographically and located in distant time zones, virtual teams are frequently composed of members drawn from different cultures who work in different organizations with unfamiliar standards and models of behavior. Lojeski and Reilly claim that lack of affinity among the team members is the greatest obstacle for getting jobs done. Reducing emotional estrangement in groups, they say, is the single most important task. Building trust can be far more difficult virtually than face-to-face. According to Richard Dool of Seton Hall, mismatches can be more easily detected in a classroom than at a distance. Dool says that team conflict often emerges out of uncertainty about tasks and roles. To mitigate ambiguity, Dool encourages virtual instructors to introduce clear team structure, with clear expectations and standards of performance. Following a three-year study of more than 250 team assignments, Dool concluded that one of the best ways to avoid conflict is for instructors to assign members to teams, rather than allowing them to decide on their own with whom they will partner.

In a chapter in *Virtual Teamwork*, a collection of essays by noted authorities, I acknowledge that teaching remotely can be unsettling: "[Instructors] can no longer rely on their ability to deliver performances that engage students intellectually and emotionally" (see Chapter 1). In traditional classrooms, instructors practice techniques that make stage actors riveting. In traditional classrooms, we're like theater-goers in front-row seats. "We are often drawn to content and energized by instructional performances." But, sadly, not all instructors are gifted. Facing dull teachers, many of us doze off, get distracted, or iPhone the class away. Online, instructors can no longer count on what they've been doing for hundreds of years. Team members are out there but, like a confident blind man tapping his way across the street, they must find their way. To stimulate virtual teams, instructors must orchestrate participants remotely, building "intellectual scaffolding," prompting students with projects, discussion topics, and questions to encourage them to think. Virtual instructors must act as facilitators, urging participants to engage in discussion and argument to generate and link ideas. Ironically, moving from physical to online space often calls upon instructors to be far more engaged than in classrooms. In virtual teams, "teaching presence" emerges from what University of Illinois professor Karen Swan identifies as engaged instructor–student interaction and feedback, exploiting e-mail, chat, discussion boards, webinars, and other applications. At their best, virtual teams work together on shared goals, not only acquiring new knowledge, but practicing how to be a talented partner—giving and receiving help, sharing and explaining content, and offering feedback. In virtual teams, personnel performs highly valued workplace skills—how to offer nuanced critique, how to challenge assumptions without alienating co-workers, how to argue your case without upsetting your peers, and especially, how to manage conflict. You not only acquire new on-the-job competencies, but you learn how to interact with others, emerging not merely as a participant, but with new roles as facilitator, reporter, and observer. Curiously, online educators say that learning online can be far more engaging than sitting passively in classrooms.

Virtual Tools

Happily, most corporations long ago introduced nearly every tool you will need to support virtual teaming across your company's footprint. At most companies, virtual teams can be launched seamlessly without introducing exotic and often expensive new hardware and software. Active at many companies, remote teams communicate in highly sophisticated ways without spending vast sums on high-end systems. Without adding a new line item in your budget and without entering negotiations with vendors, virtual teams can be set in motion at your company today, exploiting the currently installed commercial or freely available, open-source software. "Without the numerous tools and technologies now available to communicate and collaborate, virtual teams might never have become so widely successful," report the Finnish global teaching experts Anu Sivunen and Maarit Valo. Even with enhanced collaborative tools available, unsurprisingly, e-mail turns out to be the most commonly used technology. Information sharing is also supported by text-based discussion forums, usually housed on widely installed company-wide learning management systems or as part of groupware. Many products offer a variety of other common features—document distribution, live chat, among other applications. Collaboration software suites may also include calendars, application sharing, time tracking, surveys, and content and workflow management, all designed to make it easy to share information.

Peer-to-Peer Learning

Perhaps the most intriguing and productive benefit of discussion boards is their value as peer-to-peer interactive communication. In discussion forums, team members interact with one another in ways usually limited in conventional classrooms. Some experts believe that students can learn more from their peers than from absorbing lectures or reading textbooks passively. Online, members can engage in round-the-clock sharing, argument, and extended discussion, behavior rarely open to employees seated in classrooms. Blogs have emerged as a common web application, often replacing discussion forums with many of the same options, extending them by combining text, images, and hyperlinks. Teams have also adopted wikis as collaborative websites, permitting members to add and edit content.

With remote learning emerging as a highly competitive marketplace, a wide variety of meeting software is now linked to commercial learning management systems or available from vendors separately or freely on the Web. Virtual teammates can hold meetings using webinars with instructors and participants delivering real-time audio slide presentations. Webinars offer chat and "hand-raising" features aimed at stimulating engagement. Some instructors encourage employees to deliver their own webinars, giving them the chance to report on team projects in real time. Most webinars can be archived, allowing those unable to attend the option of retrieving presentations anytime. Podcasts give teams the opportunity to retrieve presentations on demand. With merely a microphone and recording software, podcasts are easily uploaded and available on mobile devices on the run. Personnel are often encouraged to produce their own podcasts to share their work with others. Because workers are often dispersed among several time zones, traveling frequently for work and family, mobile phones have largely replaced landlines. With its SMS capability, texting has transformed the nearly ubiquitous cell phone into a text-based asynchronous tool. Using Skype and other voice-over-Internet-protocol (VoIP) applications, computers now link to high-speed telephone connections with personnel able to call one another without incurring any charges. Many teams rely on teleconferencing as a common virtual-team communication tool. More recently, without introducing groupware, social networking and social media sites—such as Twitter, Facebook, and LinkedIn—give teams alternative and engaging ways of keeping in touch.

At a Sloan Foundation-sponsored workshop a top Silicon Valley chief learning office cried, "I hate e-learning." Her shocking remark opened a meeting at Stanford University. Attended by some of the industry's most prominent learning executives, most echoed disenchantment with ubiquitous plug-and-play modules used by many Fortune 500 companies. Today, innovative learning leaders are moving away rapidly from delivering isolating self-learning modules, turning instead to engaged, peer–to–peer electronic-mediated virtual classrooms. Mirroring and extending face-to-face instruction, virtual classrooms give employees the chance to participate in live or asynchronous discussions with facilitators and co-workers, interacting in creative, knowledge-building ways. While self-learning modules depend entirely on employees absorbing text and graphical elements on their own, personnel in virtual learning environments are engaged with instructors and peers in real time or through discussion threads. The key is active communication, building motivation and involvement, rather than merely absorbing facts or processes.

Guidelines

Even without a learning management system (LMS), you can run a stripped-down virtual classroom, just with e-mail and teleconferencing. Or, if you're looking for more robust collaboration tools, search the web to download free groupware. Scaling up with more sophisticated technologies offered by many companies as part of a learning suite you can introduce podcasts, video streaming, simulations, and at the high end, the extraordinary experience of telepresence. Most interactive tools give you and your learners the ability to archive lectures, presentations, and even text discussions. Digitally captured, lessons can be revisited by those who may not have absorbed key points at first. Archiving also permits learners to check in afterward to view recorded presentations they may have missed while away on assignment.

It's best to turn to your IT or training department to help you select the right communication tools. Of course, some of these, e-mail and teleconferencing for example, are commonly used, part of every worker's routine practice, and naturally, do not require training. Others, with which you may be less familiar (chat, discussion forums, blogs, webinars, wikis, and social networks), may require some help to get you up and running.

If you're the instructor, the first thing you'll want to do is post a welcome message; for example: "Hi. My name is Jane Smith, and I'm your instructor." At the start, its best to let everyone know what the course is about, how you plan to run it, how much participation you expect, and how often and when the class will meet in real time, either by teleconference, Skype, or webcasting. When they log in, learners should immediately access a brief description of your course with topics and lessons divided into modules by day or week. It's prudent to outline your expectations for participation in discussions, postings, homework, group and individual assignments and tests, among other tasks. Since most virtual classes never actually meet face-to-face, it's helpful to post useful clues about who you are (your photo and your brief profile, especially). It's also wise to encourage participants to post their photos and bios, too. It may seem counterintuitive, but learners in virtual classrooms say that they often grow closer to their peers online than in physical space, especially in corporate settings where everyone rushes off to the next assignment or to make a deadline. We've all experienced the peculiar feeling of sitting next to a co-worker for an entire course and at the end not knowing anything about her, not even her name.

Online, the most effective way of mitigating virtual distance is to stimulate peer-to-peer interaction. Assuming the role of facilitator in a text-based forum, you initiate discussion by posting a question about the topic being covered. If it's on target, your question will generate a trickle of responses at first, followed by others who may chime in, commenting on earlier posts, some disagreeing with previous conclusions. Virtual discussions can start with just a seed and grow into a giant discussion tree, branching and twigging in many directions. Your job, as a guide on the side, rather than a sage on the stage, is to enter occasionally when you see things straying or when you detect false claims or errors of fact. Otherwise, it's best to let participants learn from one another, expressing a wide range of opinions. At the close, say, at the end of the day or at the conclusion of a week-long session, you'll wrap things up succinctly, pointing out essential takeaways.

Virtual classes take students and employees seriously, placing them at the center of learning, rather than at the periphery. Workers in virtual classrooms will be prepared for some of the most challenging experiences in modern corporate life. Apart from the content they need to know, as their jobs become more complex and demanding, they will learn how to engage with others using sophisticated communication technologies, and most critically, they will learn to act effectively in teams everywhere your company does business. According to the leadership expert Michael Ryan, virtual teams have been adopted for many reasons—principally for their technological and economic advantages—but also for other key business reasons, "to enhance diversity, to engage human capital more effectively, and to pursue dynamic market possibilities." With virtual teams, says Ryan, companies can more easily open up to diverse participation. Ryan claims that diversity enhances team richness by opening up to a wide range of perspectives. Employees can now participate from practically anywhere, engaging in core business activities as well as joining strategic decision-making. "Members of global operations can now act as a single community," Ryan concludes.

Virtual Teaming in Africa and New York

Proclaiming that it "values teams within and across business units, divisions and counties," Standard Bank, a South-African financial institution—the largest in Africa—operates in 18 African and 20 other countries. It launched a virtual course for intercultural team managers, guiding participants in ways to improve virtual team effectiveness and increase productivity. It introduces team building, developing trust, cultural and linguistic barriers, and conflict resolution. Instructor-led, remote classes employ a wide range of tools—blogs, podcasts, streaming video, social networking, wikis, collaborative software, and alternate reality worlds. Personnel are free to enter anytime from anywhere, participating whenever convenient. Christine Uber Grosse, who led virtual sessions for SeaHarp Learning Solutions in Africa, said that compared with the broad possibilities open to global employees in virtual discussion, "the face-to-face linear format—where only one person can participates at a time in class discussion" now seems fairly narrow. At Standard Bank, participants agreed that, while working in a team may take more time and effort than doing things on your own, remote teamwork can be far more effective.

Across the Atlantic, Consolidated Edison of New York, the city's giant electric and gas utility, launched a major, company-wide virtual teaming effort to build a cadre of data-driven executives equipped to run the company with solid, decision-making tools. Executives, drawn from every corner of the company, engage in virtual discussions from just about anywhere—from work, at home, or even on the road. Exploiting sharply honed analytical methods, employees learn to attack seemingly intractable business problems they struggle with every day. Over time, 17 teams collaborated on solving helpdesk, recruitment, construction, and other business process problems that ultimately lent themselves dramatically to productive solutions. Investigating the steep rise in calls at the company's helpdesk, for example, the team discovered that during a five-year period, the call volume increased markedly, from 69,000 to 83,000. The length of each call also increased significantly, with an average call lasting more than six minutes. Using analytical techniques, a cross-functional virtual team collaborated on solutions to open self-service capabilities, reduce the call volume, and shorten call time. Following its study, the team proposed a number of solutions that led to the introduction of a self-service portal, customer-service training, and other interventions almost immediately. Within a few months, calls per day started to decline. Soon the number per day averaged 261. The next year, they fell to 226. Two years later, the average per day declined to 198. The next year, of more than 20,000 password inquiries, more than 17,000 were seamlessly processed by the portal. Before it was mounted, the helpdesk had fielded all of them.

Former ConEd senior vice president Luther Tai said that virtual teams, employing analytical techniques introduced in the course, produced "measurable and significant recommendations" that changed many of the utility's business processes. Tai, who participated in ConEd's first remote class, says that the success of virtual teaming was doubly valuable because it achieved company-wide objectives, "without the added travel expense and work stoppage of a conventional, on-ground classroom experience." Summing up, Tai said, "The true benefit of working virtually is the flexibility it gives employees to complete projects assignments from anywhere at any time."

Note

1   All citations in this essay are from *Virtual Teamwork*, edited by Robert Ubell, Wiley (Hoboken, NJ, 2010).

This is an edited version of a pair of essays that first appeared in T+D. "Virtual Team Learning" was first published in the August 2010 issue, pp. 53–58. "How to Run a Virtual Classroom" was published originally in October 2011.

3

ACTIVE LEARNING

Interaction, Diversity, and Evolution in Online Learning

By John Vivolo

What we once thought as the future is now the past. The ability to connect and learn in the comfort of our homes, once seen as long in the future, is now part of our everyday experience. Because next-generation learners expect technology and learning to weave together seamlessly, our dreams of the future no longer meet their needs. As a result, online learning must innovate continuously. No longer new or experimental, virtual education has become integrated as part of higher education. To succeed, it must continue to evolve.

Not since the Socratic method has education spread so widely and introduced such drastic change. Consider the growth of online learning since the introduction of broadband Internet. According to Course (2013), in the fall of 2002, online enrollments in US higher education represented merely 9.6 percent of the total. But only ten years later, college and university online enrollment reached 32 percent of degree-granting post-secondary institutions, not including MOOCs (Massive Open Online Courses). Consider the Internet itself and its ability to connect nearly everyone in the world. According to the World Wide Web Consortium (2015), an organization that tracks daily Internet usage, as of July 2016, "3,424,971,237 . . . around 40 percent of the world's population had an Internet connection" (a number that changes daily). Consider the sudden growth of Internet access over the last ten years with ". . . the first billion reached in 2005. The second billion in 2010. The third billion in 2014."

Primitive at first, online learning has reached a tipping point in higher education. Whether for-profit, non-profit, or public, schools must meet the demand of a growing student population seeking high-quality courses. The sudden appearance and popularity of MOOCs is proof enough, that students are demanding more online education. Smart universities are already making plans to develop, or at least explore, the possibility of introducing this experimental format, if merely to open a pipeline for students to enter degree-granting, traditional academic programs.

How do we fulfill next-generation student expectations for digital education that allows for continuous engagement? How do we balance the introduction of technology with methods that take the learning environment seriously? As Garrison and Kanuka (2004) comment, "It is not just finding the right mix of technologies or increasing access to learning . . . [it] is about rethinking and redesigning the teaching and learning relationship." Until recently, much of the student experience in online learning has been passive. Rather than engaging with information, students often appear to be absorbing it. Moving from passive absorption to active learning, programs must embrace digital education as interactive, diverse, and ever-evolving. As Lee and Lee (2008) remark, ". . . e-Learning is an active process of information because knowledge generation is accomplished through individual experience, maturity, and interaction with one's environment."

Enter Active Learning

While active learning exhibits many characteristics, for the purposes of this chapter, we will focus primarily on improving content presentation, increasing peer-to-peer engagement (including interactive elements), and creating a virtual learning community. Engagement and social interaction—the key elements in creating a virtual learning community—require considerable thought and planning. As McInnerney and Roberts (2004) note, "For students studying in an online environment, social interaction with peers and educators can often be an exercise in frustration. If such frustration is to be minimized, much thought needs to be given to the methods of communication that will be utilized, so that the online environment fulfills the human desire for social interaction." Introducing diverse communication tools is central to what we refer to as active learning, a digital instruction approach that balances synchronous and asynchronous communication, while preserving online learning flexibility. According to McInnerney and Roberts (2004), "Asynchronous communication may not give the immediacy that is required for successful social interaction," acknowledging that ". . . lapsed time that can occur between question and answer may not assuage the tyrannies of distance, time zones, and isolation from which learners may suffer. Isolation is not always because of distance, but often it is caused by change in the learning environment." McInnerney and Roberts (2004) recognize that ". . . even on-campus students undertaking an online course may experience a feeling of isolation from the rest of course participants." Active learning combats isolation by including video and interactive elements that help online students feel connected with "disembodied" peers they may never see. Live virtual learning (synchronous meetings) also provide opportunities to combat isolation. As with anything new, active learning must be experienced in order to adjust to it. Wegerif

(1998) recognizes that, at first, students often feel uneasy about enrolling in online courses. Many resist participating, but after engaging in a virtual community, some cross what Wegerif (1998) refers to as the threshold from "outsider" to "insider." Exploiting a diversity of communication methods, active learning can fit the needs of students new to digital education, uncertain about whether they can participate effectively. Exploiting high-quality content, coupled with interactive learning tools, active learning encourages community-building. In active learning, content is staged to elicit a certain level of student amusement. Herrington, et al. (2003) recommend that ". . . in order to fully engage with an authentic task or problem-based scenario, students need to engage with a process that is familiar to moviegoers throughout the world—suspension of disbelief." Today, online learning can exceed student expectations, engaging them in learning experiences, surprisingly different from which they have become familiar. Often built from scenario-based learning environments, active learning can provide conditions in which ". . . characters, circumstances, and parameters are drawn to simulate a real-life context for learning . . ." (Herrington, et al., 2003). While active learning generates higher quality content, its principal aim is to stimulate fluid collaborative student engagement. According to Tu and Corry (2003), "Collaborative learning engages students in knowledge-sharing, inspiring one another, depending upon one another, and applying active social interaction. Therefore, collaborative learning is an artistic, rather than mechanical process (see Chapter 1)."

The success of an active learning course depends principally on creating a learning community that adapts to the needs of individual learners. For Tu and Corry (2003), a successful online collaborative learning community supports ". . . members [who] engage intellectually, mentally, socio-cultural, and interactively in various structured and unstructured activities to achieve their common learning goals via electronic communication technologies." Continuing, Tu and Corry (2003) say that, "the main purpose of collaborative learning is to enrich learners' critical thinking, information exchange, and knowledge-generating processes and to attain rich interactive learning experiences." Tu and Corry (2003) conclude, "If learners do not see the value of collaborative learning, they will focus only on achievement and will not engage effectively in collaborative activities." To achieve results, institutions must introduce a diverse, multifaceted approach, coordinating numerous roles—instructors, faculty, instructional designers, educational technologists, trainers, student and faculty support staff, deans, managers, and directors—stimulated by "out-the-box" thinking. Building an engaging, ever-evolving program for next-generation learners is like constructing a complex machine.

Certain key technologies that make online learning possible will naturally be employed in next-generation online learning courses. Digital communication technologies—central features of an online course—giving faculty the ability to engage with students as well as giving students ways of interacting with each other, are key expectations of most students who enroll in virtual courses. According to Mupinga, et al. (2006) in one study, "The majority of online students (83 percent) expected the professor to communicate with them. If not communicating regularly, students expect 'some voice on the other end of the line,' said one student."

From the very start, when the first distance courses were launched in the early 1990s with slow, dial-up modems, until today, with modern broadband-powered courses, key technologies have been—and will remain—essential educational vehicles. But technology alone will not succeed in stimulating engaged, active learners. Rather, effective use of pedagogy—often distained by on-campus faculty—unexpectedly emerges as a first consideration in building compelling online courses. Lessons learned on how to engage remote students from the early days of online instruction—peer-to-peer and inquire-based learning, teamwork, and real-world or role-playing—have assumed even greater prominence in active learning classes. Surprisingly, institutions are just beginning to acknowledge that pedagogically innovative approaches, commonly practiced in online courses, are not often practiced on campus. According to Prince (2004), "Active Learning is generally defined as any instructional method that engages students in the learning process." Prince continues, "In short, active learning requires students to do meaningful learning activities and think about what they are doing."

Evolving from passive learning in many online programs, faculty are recognizing the need to introduce active and engaging course activities, aligned with student cognitive learning processes that give students opportunities for creative participation as well as enjoyment. As Prince (2004) remarks, "Active learning is often contrasted to the traditional lecture where students passively receive information from the instructor" (see Chapter 5). Next-generation learners no longer view technology as a luxury, but have adopted it as a necessity. Students now demand that digital education meet their expectations for mobile, accessible, fast, interactive, and never-passive learning. When next-generation learners roll out of bed, they are unlikely to grab a textbook; instead, they reach for a phone or tablet. The heart of active learning requires a push-and-pull balance of interactive and active, asynchronous and synchronous content and communication methods. Expectations are high, and higher education must meet that challenge. Evolve or die.

Not based on a specific technology, active learning is a method for developing and managing online courses. This chapter offers general suggestions on types of technologies to help online course builders meet the requirements of introducing active learning.

Active Learning Framework

In building an active learning online course, it's best to recognize two fundamental perspectives in any course, whether on campus or online. Consider these two views:

Holistic view focuses on learning objectives and topics presented each "week," and

Structural view, revealing how a course has been taught on campus and how to employ those elements as building blocks to migrate online.

From a structural perspective, when learning objectives remain largely the same, both on campus or online, faculty must reimagine how the on-campus course is to be delivered in an online environment. Once faculty and instructional designers engage in purposeful discussions and arrive at a mutual understanding of the course's learning objectives, the team must then explore the structure of the course. The first step is to appreciate the format instructors employ in their on-campus classes. Excluding labs and high-stakes assignments, normally performed outside of class, we are left with three basic elements that comprise most on-campus classes:

- Lectures
- In-class discussions
- In-class, low-stakes assignments, quizzes, etc.

On-campus *lectures* range anywhere from ten-minute overviews to two hours or more. While instructional designers encourage short bursts, the length of an online lecture depends entirely on the content the instructor wishes to impart. Engineering or science courses often require longer lectures than those in the arts and social sciences. While any subject can be chunked and reimagined, engineering may resist chunking because instructors often allow little or no time for discussion or debate, other than clarification in a question or two. Let's imagine that an instructor lectures about 30 minutes each week in a three-hour, on-campus course. (We will calculate the remaining time as we go along.)

Next, let's look at the *discussion*. A staple of any class, discussion is the oldest tool in any online learning course, but also one that gives developers the most difficulty. How do we replicate the personal experiences, generated between student and student and faculty and student that occur on campus, if participants are not present in the same room? They may not even be in the same city, state or country. In a conventional, on-campus class, discussion time may take one and a half hours. Earlier, in our example, we calculated that the lecture component covered 30 minutes; adding the discussion, we now can account for two hours of our three-hour course.

Finally, let's consider low-stakes *quizzing, assignments, group work or projects* and other elements that comprise many face-to-face classes. These components fill the remaining hour, bringing us to a total of three hours. During a group project or presentation, discussion and in-class assignments may intermingle, making it difficult to separate them into discrete elements. Because each class is unique, divisions in this example are arbitrary in order to establish a theoretical model. Remember that while digital education allows for far more instructional flexibility than on-campus classes, curiously, most schools, accrediting bodies, and state education authorities still require a specific number of hours devoted to instruction, even in an online course (see Chapter 4). The purpose of this model is to help faculty move from an on-campus to online course. But once we have established the model, our next objective is to deconstruct it, unpacking conventional on-campus instruction, by moving away from it to introduce nonlinear pedagogical thinking, better suited to active learning in a virtual course.

Appreciating the general structure of an on-campus course, we can now explore how our understanding can help us convert each part into online active-learning instruction. In building an active-learning course, it's useful to consider an online course as having these three principal components:

- Interactive Adaptive Modules (IAMs)
- Advanced Discussion Boards (ADBs)
- Live Virtual Learning Sessions (LVL)

Interactive Adaptive Modules (IAMs)

Before the introduction of virtual active-learning courses, traditional online courses were built using audio and video files, together with text and graphic elements, employing commercial applications, such as Microsoft PowerPoint, Word, Excel, and other text- and graphic-based formats, in addition to video and audio recordings. Commonly, conventional online courses rely principally on one or two of these items—PowerPoint with audio and animation. In contrast, active learning exploits as many formats as possible, containing them in an easily reconfigured "bucket" (or module), as we will call them.

Consider IAMs as virtual containers or modules (that may use a SCORM[1] player) to create "Scenes[2]." Using an Online Learning Storyboard[3], these Scenes can follow a sample path, illustrated by this example:

> **Scene 1:** In an introduction, say, of no more than a few minutes, the instructor delivers a high-definition video message, reviewing the previous session, together with an outline of the module's learning objectives (Figure 3.1).
>
> **Scene 2:** A quick interactive quiz, reviewing the previous session's content (often a non-graded assignment, but with a required completion before students are permitted to move forward) (Figure 3.2).
>
> **Scene 3:** This scene relies on a concept, easily outlined in a storyboard or case study, in a visual format. Emphasizing visual representation of content with minimal text, it is presented using high-definition audio recordings delivered over a slide presentation. Visual elements encourage interactive responses, giving the learner a narrative connection to the content. It also

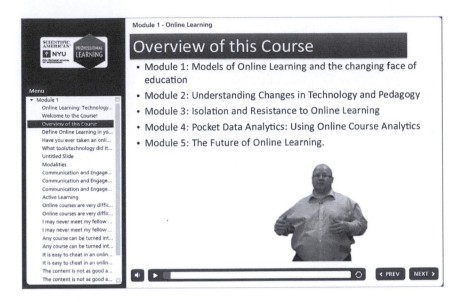

Figure 3.1

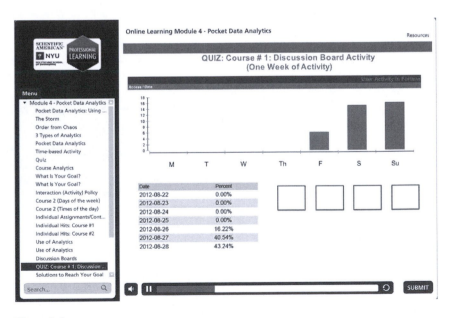

Figure 3.2

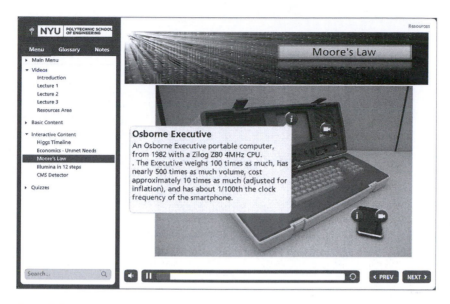

Figure 3.3

provides engaging, entertaining elements to stimulate student attention (Figure 3.3).

Scene 4: This interactive learning element shows an on-screen object, layered with data in various formats, that asks learners to interact with it by touching the screen, moving graphical elements, or performing other simple activities on screen. The goal is not to encourage complex inter-actions, but to give students opportunities to engage with a simple object, such as an image or graphic. In one example, students are shown a timeline on the screen, commonly a flat image with points of interest along the way. The student is then asked to complete the timeline, manipulating points on the timeline with various elements—audio, pop-up videos, articles, and other layers of information—that populate the timeline, exploring various options at the learner's own pace (Figure 3.4).

Scene 5: Another video of the instructor appears. While active learning is best when students are not exposed to too many videos, still, it's wise to intersperse your IAM with occasional faculty videos. While entirely the devel-oper's personal preference, it's recommended that you introduce a "pop-in" faculty video every three or four scenes to provide students with guidance on the next topic or scene. Interpersonal connections between student and faculty helps humanize the online learning experience (Figure 3.5).

Figure 3.4

Figure 3.5

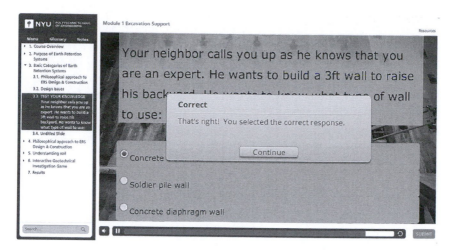

Figure 3.6

Scene 6: Quiz or Lab. Low-stakes quizzing or labs are shorter, chunked learning elements. Pre- and post-topic quizzing reinforces knowledge acquired and improves student learning (Figure 3.6).

Scene 7: Additional scenes. Extending delivery by introducing additional scenes hinges on the extent of the content you wish to cover. Assuming you create 20–60 minute IAMs, then you will need to offer extra scenes.

The IAM (scene) format allows for great flexibility—any element can be replaced, swapped with another, extended or abbreviated to meet the needs of the content delivered, student response, or faculty requirements. As a result, IAMs are ever-evolving and constantly adapting to the needs of students and faculty (see Chapter 4).

Interactive Adaptive Module Technology

Technology is a fickle thing that changes constantly. Because of its variability, it meets the needs of IAMs for flexibility. IAMs are not wedded to any particular piece of technology, but can easily be adapted to a variety of currently available digital authoring tools. Tools you select should give you the flexibility to modify weekly presentations quickly, so that they can be connected easily to video, audio, and other files. At their best, modules adapt to real-time, in-semester analytics, surveys, or other student and faculty needs. Technological diversity is at the heart of IAMs.

High-quality IAMs depend on high-quality audio and video files. Today, it is relatively easy to record high-quality, high-definition video with easily affordable cameras. Editing a video, which was once difficult, is a skill that is now comparatively simple to acquire from free tutorials on public video-sharing sites. Free editing tools are available as part of many cloud-sharing packages. Even Ultra Keying (green-screen editing) is relatively easy to master. With many eLearning-authoring tools, you can now introduce animation without tangling with complex programs.

Advanced Discussion Boards (ADBs)

Engagement and peer-to-peer learning is at the heart of active learning. While IAMs provide robust, interactive modules and low-stake quizzing, they remain self-paced, without student interaction with their peers. The need for asynchronous communication is central to active learning. Discussion boards have existed since the very start of online learning. They are found in nearly every online course, and undoubtedly, they will continue to be employed because of their ease of use and enormous educational benefits. Every learning management system (LMS) offers a discussion board as part of its suite of applications. But owing to advances in technology and pedagogy, this timeworn tool can now move to a more robust level of communication. Next-generation learner expectations and social media are driving discussion boards to move beyond simple text. With quick audio and video responses available to most students, online discussions must adapt. As Garrison and Kanuka (2004) note, "A source of this transformation stems from the ability of online learners to be both together and apart and to be connected to a community of learners anytime and anywhere, without being time-, place-, or situation-bound." While advanced discussion boards still rely primarily on text, other communication formats are vying for a place. Most discussion-board tools in LMSs now offer a number of other communication options.

Advanced Discussion Board Options

Audio recordings can be stored in your LMS server or can be embedded in an audio-or-video hosting site.

Video recordings can be stored in your server or embedded in a video-sharing site. Most video-sharing sites commonly offer three options—video uploading, webcam recording, and screen-sharing. The latter now allows for highly technical classes, like those in computer science, to display what is on student or faculty screens, with a voice-over or small-screen video embedded next to the screen capture.

HTML Coding Discussion boards can employ html source-coding to help create a rich visual experience that displays websites, rather than merely the text drawn from a discussion board.

As online learning tools evolve, discussion forums are undergoing vast improvements, with techniques that not only exploit the science of communication, but its art.

Live Virtual Learning Sessions

"Connection with others is essential to realize a community of inquiry characterized by reflective written or spontaneous verbal dialogue," report Garrison and Kanuka (2004). Lack of student-to-student and faculty-to-student engagement is one of the reasons many say they refuse to teach or take courses online. Resistance is understandable, since our educational and professional lives are heightened by communicating with each other in real time (see Chapter 5). In many virtual classes, however, we are expected to learn on our own without "live" guidance. While asynchronous learning, especially interactive modules encourage engaged learning, real-time live interaction is often missing. "Dialogue is an important element of all teaching and learning, but in distance education it presents a challenge," comment McBrien, et al. (2009) encouraging synchronous dialog to "... empower students in conversation and expression. Many of these students never initiate comments in the traditional classroom."

While the present technology gives users simple ways to introduce live or blended components in an online class, only recently can instructors incorporate real-time events into virtual courses. Much of the early resistance to online education may have derived from the failure of primitive technologies to achieve robust communication. Even recently, hosting a synchronous event in an online class was a challenge, often driving faculty and students away. Tools were clunky, requiring complex "wizards" to implement audio and video communication. Luckily, today, there is a vast array of easy-to-install, simple applications. Here are some potential live virtual learning options available today:

Chat Rooms If you can say something is "traditional" in online learning, you may call chat rooms "traditional." One of the older synchronous tools—together with its cousin, instant messenger—chat rooms allow for near real-time messaging between participants. Other than sending links, images, and short videos, however, its diversity pretty much ends there. Nonetheless, it is a good tool for those with limited bandwidth and constrained financial means.

Virtual Classrooms A chat room with more "bells and whistles," virtual classrooms provide more engagement, with document uploading and drawing tools that permit engagement beyond simply text-messaging.

Videoconferencing Digital video cameras in the form of webcams give faculty and students the ability to enter live conversations. With Voice Over Internet Protocol (VoIP), videoconferencing gives you the flexibility of hosting virtual office hours, often limited to video and with some sharing.

Webinars Increasingly exploited as part of virtual classes, webinars bundle a number of tools that are close to replicating in-person experience. Multiple webcam sharing (sometimes up to 25 at once), plus screen-sharing, document uploading, chat rooms, phone lines, VoIP, and other group collaboration tools give webinars the potential to deliver a complete learning experience. More than just hosting office hours, faculty can now orchestrate classroom sessions, lectures, group presentations, quizzing, projects, etc. But owing to the constraints of bit rates in current webinar systems, webcams have limitations, even high-definition webcams, since they fail to offer truly clear video.

Live Streaming The next step toward a fully robust, real-time solution is high-quality live streaming video, permitting bit rates of more than 2,500, resulting in amazingly clear video. Coupled with high-quality computers and inserted rendering cards, your class can now experience faithful live images.

Days of Future Present

What will the expectations of online students be in 10–20 years? How do we meet their expectations pedagogically and technologically? As more institutions accept online learning as a standard practice, the need to adopt more engaging and interactive learning methods will become increasingly obvious. Active learning encourages a constant state of evolution that closely follows rapid technological advances as well as the acceptance of more innovative pedagogies. Technical and pedagogical apparatus we once hoped would be waiting for us in the future are now a part of our present learning toolbox. Active learning gives us the freedom we never thought possible in our lifetimes. As Gerdy (1998–1999) remarks, "Good learning, like good work, is collaborative and social, not competitive and isolated; sharing one's ideas and responding to others' ideas, improves thinking and deepens understanding"—the goal of active learning for the next-generation online learning students.

Notes

1   SCORM: Standard Content Object Reference Module. This format is designed to function as an interactive tool that connects to most eLearning authoring tools and management systems.
2   Scenes: Much like a movie, a scene is a section of learning that is self-contained, focusing on learning objectives. It can contain various objects, such as video, audio, and quizzing, always pin-pointing a single learning objective. Scenes take the place of on-campus lectures, as well as some low-stakes assignments or quizzes.
3   Online Learning Storyboard: Online course developers and instructional designers outline a plan, describing how scenes will support learning objectives. The scene also functions as a blueprint for course building, allowing instructional designers to use the course developer's notes to create an interactive and engaging course.

References

Allen, I. E. & Seaman, J. (2013) *Changing Course: Ten Years of Tracking Online Education in the United States*. Newburyport, MA: Sloan Consortium.

Garrison, D. R. & Kanuka, H. (2004). Blended learning: Uncovering its transformative potential in higher education. *The Internet and higher education*, 7(2), 95–105.

Gerdy, K. B. (1998–1999). *If Socrates only knew: Expanding law class discourse*. Reuben Clark Law School, Brigham Young University. Lawyering Skills Section 9.

Herrington, J., Oliver, R. & Reeves, T. C. (2003). Patterns of engagement in authentic online learning environments. *Australasian Journal of Educational Technology*, 19(1).

Konstantakos, D. (2015). *Module 1: Excavation support: Course overview*. Retrieved from NYU Tandon School of Engineering. Figure 4 and 6. NYU Classes: Newclasses.nyu.edu.

Lee, J. K. & Lee, W. K. (2008). The relationship of e-Learner's self-regulatory efficacy and perception of e-Learning environmental quality. *Computers in Human Behavior*, 24(1), 32–47.

McBrien, J. L., Cheng, R., & Jones, P. (2009). Virtual spaces: Employing a synchronous online classroom to facilitate student engagement in online learning. *The International Review of Research in Open and Distributed Learning*, 10(3), 3–4.

McInnerney, J. M. & Roberts, T. S. (2004). Online learning: Social interaction and the creation of a sense of community. *Journal of Educational Technology & Society*, 7(3), 73–81.

Mupinga, D. M., Nora, R. T., & Yaw, D. C. (2006). The learning styles, expectations, and needs of online students. *College teaching*, 54(1), 185–189.

Prince, M. (2004). Does active learning work? A review of the research. *Journal of Engineering Education-Washington*, 93, 223–232.

Stern, R. (2015). *Lecture 17: Programmable chips*. Retrieved from NYU Tandon School of Engineering, Digital Logic and State Machine Design. Figure 5. NYU Classes: Newclasses.nyu.edu.

Tu, C. H. & Corry, M. (2003). Building active online interaction via a collaborative learning community. *Computers in the Schools*, 20(3), 51–59.

Vivolo, J. (2015). *Module 1: The evolution online learning*. Retrieved from NYU Tandon School of Engineering and Scientific American, Online Learning: Technology and the Future of Education. Figure 1. NYU Classes: Newclasses.nyu.edu.

Vivolo, J. (2015). *Module 4: Pocket data analytics*. Retrieved from NYU Tandon School of Engineering and Scientific American, Online Learning: Technology and the Future of Education. Figure 2. NYU Classes: Newclasses.nyu.edu.

Vivolo, J. (2015). *Module 1: Sample interactive learning modules*. Retrieved from NYU Tandon School of Engineering. Figure 3. NYU Classes: Newclasses.nyu.edu.

Wegerif, R. (1998). The social dimension of asynchronous learning networks. *Journal of asynchronous learning networks*, 2(1), 34–49.

World Wide Web Consortium. (August 2015). Retrieved from Internetlivesstats.com.

This essay on Active Learning is by John Vivolo, Director of Online and Virtual Learning, NYU Tandon School of Engineering, written expressly for this volume.

4

WHAT YOU CAN DO ONLINE, BUT NOT ON CAMPUS

Most of us believe that online education is far less accommodating and flexible than on-campus classes. From childhood, we know that classrooms bring us face-to-face with other students and our teachers, giving us direct access to how they look, what they say, how they think, and how we feel about them. Sitting at desks or moving about, our bodies and minds inhabit the classroom, often with the same ease and familiarity we find at home. Most of us assume it's the ideal learning environment.

But the classroom may not be as hospitable as we imagine. Looking at certain online pedagogical practices, we may discover there are other ways that may enhance learning beyond what is possible inside four walls. While at first, the schoolroom seems to allow us a full range of possibilities, unexpectedly, when we look inside, we may find there are ways it may inhibit learning. Despite our deep affinity with the schoolroom, it turns out that it can be unanticipatedly restrictive. Turning conventional wisdom on its head, let's consider digital pedagogical strategies, not commonly found in the schoolroom that may be highly productive online.

Anonymity

Stepping into your class on campus, you're on display—everybody sees you and can easily form an impression of who they imagine you are, perceptions based merely on how you look. Your classmates immediately know your gender, your race, and can make a good guess about many of your other attributes, based on what they see—your age, for example, and other obvious characteristics. They know whether you're tall or overweight, the color of your hair and eyes, or if you're physically challenged. Long before you speak, your presence presents your instructor and your peers with a complex, if quite limited, picture of who they think you are. As the semester progresses, you walk into your class each week as if you're a character in *Cheers* where everybody knows your name.

As you navigate remote domains on the Web, if you use a pseudonym, you can sink entirely out of sight, leaving hardly a trace, falling into complete anonymity. In an online class, however, your identity is only partially obscured, moving in and out of observation like a figure seen from behind a foggy glass. As a student enrolled in a virtual course, following the same protocols required of on-campus students, your name is automatically posted, visible to your virtual instructor and classmates. If you have a common given name—like Tom or Jane— everyone knows if you're a man or a woman. Some names are ambiguous. "Michael," for example, can be male or female and transgender students add another identity that may not fall clearly into a gender divide. Asian, Middle Eastern, African, and others around the world may possess names that cannot be identified easily. In some virtual classes, faculty ask students to mount their digital portraits and post brief biographies. In other online classes, video and other technologies unmask your virtual identity, displaying images of students participating in webinars and other real-time or archived activities.

Unexpectedly, in a digital course, despite the fact that your classmates may know your name, gender, and other things about you, because you are obscured from total view, you and others in your virtual class act *as if* you're anonymous. On campus, because you are fully visible, you are subject to the same attitudes people have outside of class about your identity—your gender, age, sexuality, race, ethnicity, and religion, as well as your political opinions, social and economic class, disability, language, nationality, and other characteristics.

"With an online course, nobody knows who you really are," recalled an African-American student who works for the Tennessee Board of Regents. "They don't know your ethnicity unless you have a picture on your profile. I felt like, I can do this. There is no one stereotyping me" (Haynie, 2014). As a 49-year-old single mother from Nashville, Tennessee, she was always aware of her race in college, feeling that others were judging her for her dark skin. But in her online class at a Tennessee university, she was comfortable with her digital classmates— and her skin color—in ways she never felt on campus.

Strikingly, partial invisibility online gives students a license to express themselves more openly than they would on campus (Suler, 2004). Known as the *online disinhibition effect*, it allows students to abandon conventional social restrictions commonly present face-to-face. According to psychologist John Suler, virtual students often feel more comfortable revealing private thoughts and feelings than they do in conventional classrooms. On campus, some students report that they often hesitate to communicate directly with faculty, but online they feel they can ask questions of their instructors far more easily. Students who avoid participation in class say they fear criticism or worry about making mistakes (Caspi, et al. 2006). The online disinhibition effect lowers common psychological restraints that tend to regulate online behavior. Characterized by reduced inhibitions and a lowered regard for social boundaries in cyberspace, it can be expressed in positive or negative ways. Online, a few exploit partial invisibility by acting aggressively, with rude language, harsh criticism and other antisocial behavior, known as "cyberbullying." While more common in social media, cyberbullying in virtual classes can still be unsettling. Luckily, it is not often encountered in digital courses but should troublesome online students disrupt your class, faculty can manage things professionally and respectfully by issuing calm but firm warnings, alerting students to university rules that prohibit disruptive behavior. Rarely are serious repercussions enforced.

Visual anonymity can serve as a shield, allowing more equal participation, reducing hierarchical differences. In daily life, you can often tell who hold positions of status by the way they dress, how they carry themselves, the way they speak, among other easily acknowledged signs of authority. Online, however, nearly all these cues fall away. Since everyone online participates on an equal footing, no matter how influential some are, their authority in virtual space carries much less weight. "Everyone—regardless of status, wealth, race, or gender—starts off on a level playing field," notes Suler about the virtual environment. In your digital course, your communicating skills, competence, intelligence, and technical proficiency are what count; your standing elsewhere is of far less importance. "People are reluctant to say what they really think as they stand before an authority figure," observes Suler. "But online, in what feels more like a peer relationship—with the appearances of authority minimized—people are much more willing to speak out . . .." Online, anonymity and unidentifiability may reduce inhibitions caused by social anxiety, freeing shy students to enter into more frequent personal interactions, with a greater likelihood of forming closer relationships than they would on-campus. As Israeli scholars Noam Lapidot-Lefler and Azy Barak conclude, "The perception of anonymity and unidentifiability over the Internet gives the user a sense of control over the degree of self-disclosure, in terms of extent, time, and place, which leads to heightened intimacy and openness" (Lapidot-Lefle, 2015).

Secured behind a mask of concealed identity, anonymity has protected citizens for centuries, allowing people to act without worry. In an egalitarian society, it is also among our most treasured possessions, permitting us to participate in some of our most socially valuable institutions—peer review, whistle-blowing, voting. In virtual classes, "[a]nonymity may encourage freedom of thought and expression by promising people a possibility to express opinions and develop arguments about positions that, for fear of reprisal or ridicule, they would not or dare not take otherwise," (Nissenbaum, 1999) says NYU privacy scholar Helen Nissenbaum.

"Anonymity has played a central role in conflicts over freedom and individual liberty, but not until the introduction of the Internet has it become as widely acknowledged as a citizen's right," remarks Malcolm Collins, co-founder of ArtCorgi.com. "Without anonymity, Deep Throat would have been impossible as a check on corruption within the Executive Branch. The formation of the US government was heavily influenced by anonymous debates undertook via the *Federalist Papers*. Even the American Revolution was partially instigated by the anonymously published pamphlet, *Common Sense*. Without the protection offered by anonymity, the US would be a radically different country" (Collins, 2013).

On the Internet, most users expect your offline and online identity to be disconnected, with anonymity common in most online communities other than those—like Facebook and LinkedIn—that facilitate offline socialization. "Within almost all online communities, it is seen as offensive to demand even basic information on a user's real-world identity (such as sex, race, location, etc.)," says Collins. "Within online communities, anonymity has become increasingly associated with the maintenance of a free society. Anonymity is seen as allowing for discussion in environments in which a person's input is judged solely by its merit and untainted by other participants' biases with regard to that person's sex, formal education, ethnicity, income, age, or culture of origin."

Anonymity is closely linked to our notion of privacy in which a person has "basic rights to pursue one's own values free from the impingement of others (DeCew, 2015)." Privacy, according to UCLA political scientist Robert Gerstein, allows us to live our lives without intrusion or observation—to experience life spontaneously, without shame (Gerstein, 1978). Obscured by partial anonymity, online students escape the bright light of exposure in conventional classes. The student in a virtual environment is like a patient in psychoanalysis. On the couch, the patient's gaze is turned away from the analyst, with the doctor draped in a zone of anonymity—heard but not seen—freeing the patient to express herself in ways she might not when facing her therapist. Similar behavior is experienced by people who say intimate, often secret, confessions to strangers on a bus or airplane. The disinhibition effect operates effectively in digital courses, permitting students to explore unconventional trains of thought they may be hesitant to pursue on campus—fearing conflict, rejection, even contempt, or worse, ridicule. We all know from our own unsteady feelings—vulnerability, competition, inadequacy—when all eyes turn on us in class, you can swallow your potentially risky thoughts, burying them in your throat in silence.

Learning Analytics

Unless you videotape your on-campus class, what happens inside the schoolroom is rarely captured, except by frenzied students who take obsessive notes. Like water running from a tap down the drain, on-campus student data disappears at the end of each class, escaping the process of gathering and measuring what goes on. In most fields of inquiry, the goal of data collection is to capture quality evidence, allowing investigators to respond convincingly to questions that have been posed. While schools routinely collect vast amounts of data about course completion, graduation and retention rates, and other measures of student and school performance, reliable information about what actually happens inside the classroom is essentially missing. In contrast, online, nearly every action and interaction can be captured. Using learning analytic software, every moment can be secured, collected, and displayed, open to inspection and analysis.

As a field of inquiry, learning analytics emerges from data drawn from course management systems and other educational software that uncover digital evidence generated by students and faculty in virtual classes. Learning management systems —now almost universally installed in every class in the nation's universities— routinely track online student participation, monitoring discussion-board postings, following student access to digital materials, quiz results, assessments, and other elements (Picciano, 2012). The results can predict future student performance, provide students with personalized learning pathways, or intervene on behalf of students at risk or in need of faculty guidance. Some learning software display data visually on learning "dashboards," providing students and instructors with a graphical presentation of findings. As an interdisciplinary domain, learning analytics draws on such well-established scholarly areas as statistics, data mining, artificial intelligence, social network analysis, visualization, and machine learning, among other fields.

In astronomy, the object of study is knowledge of heavenly bodies. Focusing telescopes on the moon, for example, scientists collect data to gain insights into its characteristics. In education, the object of study is student learning, but until digital means of gathering data was introduced recently with educational software, little or no data emerged directly from the classroom, the very site where institutional learning occurs. For thousands of years, lacking proper tools to study what actually happens, the classroom remained a black box. "Before the advent of computers, exactly what materials students looked at, and how long they spent reviewing each item, was unknown to professors, and seemed unknowable," comments reporter Jeffery R. Young in *The Chronicle of Higher Education* (Young, 2016).

While lecture-capture technology is available at many schools, cameras record content delivered by instructors—classroom *teaching*—not student behavior, participation, outcomes, or other data reflecting student *learning*. On campus, you don't know if students have read the last chapter or how often they watched a video clip. Without substantive data, teachers cannot intervene until tests are graded or papers are read. Even then, faculty have no idea how students will fare on their next exam or how they will do in the course.

In sharp contrast to the empty data file on campus, online instructors have access to a continuous flow of student data. *Campus Technology* editor Mary Grush found that there are three main ways of forecasting how students will do—how often they log on to their course, how often they read or engage with course materials, and practice exercises, and how they do on assignments. Grush claims that faculty can predict, after the first week of a course, with 70 percent accuracy, whether students will complete the course successfully (Grush, 2011). By identifying level of risk for every student, learning analytics allow instructors, advisors, and support staff to move in quickly to help those most at risk. To avoid being overwhelmed by a flood of data, my colleague, John Vivolo at NYU's Tandon School of Engineering, proposes that online instructors focus on limited patterns of student behavior, say, in a single virtual course, rather than digging through large-scale data sets. Vivolo recommends that faculty can get a good idea of learner performance by examining student data during a targeted period, perhaps over a week, exploiting course analytics as a practical tool to provide online student support (Vivolo, 2014).

Without data to guide them, faculty can only guess which parts of their classroom instruction are effective. Was last week's lecture on track? Is this slide too complex? Should the class begin with an overview? Or should you plunge right in? In face-to-face instruction, faculty are often puzzled over what works and what doesn't. If they feel they're not getting through, the most common recourse is to wait until the next semester to try something different to fix it. Instead, digital learning analytics can be a productive academic force, driving continuous improvement by revealing how students actually navigate through an online course. Data can show which elements students may ignore, for example, and which ones they may find puzzling or difficult. Using results drawn from student-use data, instructors can modify the curriculum by restructuring content to make it more accessible or hone language in exam questions to increase chances of student success. To give learners greater flexibility, matching options with learner styles, some faculty test student outcomes against various delivery modes—text-based documents, audio lectures, slide presentations, or video streaming—uncovering which approach might be effective or, perhaps most innovative, whether students do best by accessing a wide variety of delivery modes. In active learning (see Chapter 3), course modules can be reassembled, altered, inserted, or deleted, measuring which ones are most successful.

Learning analytics is a core property of adaptive learning, an interactive teaching method, derived from a cross-fertilization of artificial intelligence, cognitive psychology, and learning science. In the blossoming education technology industry, largely spawned by recent advances in digital learning coupled with adaptive methods, the giant publishing house Pearson has partnered with Knewton to deliver personalized adaptive services. The company claims it "Helps teachers guide each student along their own best path through the material" (www.knewton.com/approach/). Similarly, McGraw Hill's ALEKS (Assessment and Learning in Knowledge Spaces) says that it provides students with an "individualized learning experience tailored to their unique strengths and weaknesses" (www.aleks.com/highered). Introduced mostly in math and science online and remedial courses, advocates claim it can break the "iron triangle" of cost, access, and quality by substituting technology for faculty. "Some of this may be overstated and overblown, as the up-front investment for adaptive technology is still beyond what most institutions can afford, especially given the long-term payoff is still largely unproven" (Fleming, 2014).

According to a report issued by the US Department of Education, learning analytics can be used to build models to reveal "what a learner knows, what a learner's behavior and motivation are, what the user experience is like, and how satisfied users are with online learning . . .. Because these data are gathered in real time, there is a real possibility of continuous improvement via multiple feedback loops that operate at different time scales—immediate to the student for the next problem, daily to the teacher for the next day's teaching, monthly to the principal for judging progress, and annually to the district and state administrators for overall school improvement" (Marie, et al., 2012).

A major concern raised by learning analytics, however, is how faculty and institutions maintain the confidentiality of student data. Personal information can be disclosed inadvertently, or worse, revealed by design, say, when sold to commercial vendors without student permission. To protect learner data, universities must introduce formal policies that guarantee that students own the rights to their data generated in online classes, that they have the right to correct errors posted in their files, and that they have control over how schools share their data with others.

Writing

The schoolroom is a place where the spoken word is the principal means of communication among classmates and between students and faculty. Except for note-taking, quizzes, exams, and in rare other occasions, writing is largely performed elsewhere—at home, library, and other locations outside of class to produce homework assignments, term papers, or other documents. Communication theorists Anne-Laure Fayard and Anca Metiu note that despite the crucial importance of writing in modern life, "a tacit assumption persists: that face-to-face interaction is the ideal, richest form of communication and that nothing can replace it . . . we tend to perceive face-to-face communication as 'truer' and deeper, more authentic, more genuine" (Fayard & Metiu, 2013). Delivered quickly in real-time, speech has often been thought of as the most basic form of communication, expressing thoughts and feelings most directly.

In contrast, online discussions are carried on almost entirely in text—in digital message boards forums, by e-mail, through social media, and other peer-to-peer conversations, held as if participants were writing digital letters to one another. Fayard and Metiu say that e-mail and other forms of digital communication have revived the creative dynamism often found in traditional correspondence among notable scholars. They claim that important advances were stimulated by intense exchanges of letters between key figures in science—Darwin, Einstein, and Freud—with close colleagues.

Writing is at the center of our culture. It is the core of literature, science, philosophy, commerce; practically no aspect of modern society is sustainable without it. Before the invention of writing, knowledge was transmitted orally, allowing the accumulation of thought to be passed along haphazardly or lost. Writing permits knowledge transfer, giving us the ability to capture, organize, create, and distribute it to others. In scholarship, commerce, and other spheres, your intellectual achievement is judged almost entirely by the quality and extent of your written words. When speaking in class, your thoughts are delivered in real-time, extemporaneously and unfiltered, subject to your shifting mood and porous memory; unless recorded, they disappear, evaporating like ghosts. With writing, you can structure your thoughts and clarify your ideas. Writing permits you to gather data, arguments, and experiences drawn from other sources and combine them into a reasoned text, giving others time to reflect and comment intelligently. "From their first-day introductions of themselves to their final journal reflections on the class, the vast majority of student work takes the form of considered, thoughtful prose," comments Prof. Gregory Semenza of the University of Connecticut about his virtual students (Semenza, 2015).

Reflection

Bound by four walls, the classroom is not only a confined place, but it is also restricted by time, limiting student interaction to the "credit hour," an academic unit—imposed on universities since the late nineteenth century—curbing student engagement to a defined period. Rather than measuring student learning, the credit hour arbitrarily uses time as the basis for judging educational attainment. The Carnegie Unit[1] (or student hour) forms the basis, not only of determining when classes begin and end, but also provides evidence of course completion and, ultimately, even the foundation for awarding academic degrees. Faculty workload and evaluation are also judged by the same yardstick. It is a late Victorian economic model—employed universally in the US as it was more than a century ago—as a standard for calculating faculty compensation, paralleling the way factory workers are paid by the hour, oddly applied today in every course delivered at every college and university in the US.

As Arthur Levine, former President of Columbia University's Teachers College, comments,

> The concern in colleges and schools is shifting from teaching to learning—what students know and can do, not how long they are taught. Education at all levels is becoming more individualized, as students learn different subjects at different rates and learn best using different methods of instruction . . . Today, schools and colleges are being required to use the fixed-process, fixed-calendar and Carnegie Unit accounting system of the industrial era
> (Levine, 2015).

Accreditors and state education agencies still hold digital classes to the same standard, requiring online programs to follow the same number of credit hours as on campus, ignoring the fact that faculty and students online can easily leap over barriers of space and time. Knowing the bell won't ring, virtual students often engage in discussion long past the clock, participating in forums for hours, occasionally over days. Making sure the class doesn't run over, conventional instructors limit class discussion when the bell rings. The schoolroom—like so many other spheres of life—falls under the discipline of time. The conventional classroom is often ruled by the clock, whose hands act like a pair of scissors, cutting off thought.

On-campus, faculty routinely engage students in question-and-answer volleys, reminiscent of *Jeopardy*, with the object of the game to give a correct answer, not to explore possible alternatives or raise doubts. In grade school, we learned how to perform the question-and-answer act, sitting dutifully in our seats, waiting for the teacher to toss a question. Arms shoot up, hands wave. If you were among the lucky ones, you were chosen. Luckier still, if you gave the right answer, followed by a rewarding smile from the teacher and relief from the rest of the class, freed from the anxiety of coming up with a response. Unless you're a student in a small seminar, where complex, thoughtful discussion is encouraged, similar educational charades are performed every day in classrooms everywhere, with the teacher concluding that the student who gave the right answer actually mastered something. Very likely, however, the eager student who hit on the correct answer learned nothing. In giving her response, she may just be parroting what she already knew. As for the rest of the class, it's unclear whether they learned anything either, since there is no guarantee that hearing an answer imparts knowledge, especially if the other students didn't understand the question. Encouraging speed over reflection, many instructors urge students to deliver quick responses. The student whose hand goes up first is often favored over those who need time to reflect, who may be weighing various alternatives thoughtfully. "Direct, immediate discharge or expression of an impulsive tendency is fatal to thinking" (Reflective Thinking, 2015).

"In any face-to-face classroom," notes Prof. Semenza," a small number of students emerge as truly skillful participants, speaking not just regularly, but also eloquently, while others speak only out of a sense of obligation, and many don't speak at all" (Semenza, 2015). Echoing Semenza, online instructor Mark Kassop notes that on campus

> the instructor asks a question, and the same four or five extroverted students inevitably raise their hands. They offer spontaneous, often unresearched responses in the limited time allotted for discussion. In the online environment, discussions enter a new dimension. When an instructor posts a question on the asynchronous discussion board, every student in the class is expected to respond, respond intelligently, and respond several times.
>
> (Kassop, 2003)

"As a result," Kassop continues, "students have the opportunity to post well-considered comments without the demands of the immediate, anxiety-producing, face-to-face discussion, which often elicits the first response that comes to mind rather than the best possible response."

Confirming Semenza's and Kassop's experience, sociologists David Karp and William Yoels found that in traditional classes with more than 40 students, only two to three students accounted for about half of all student comments (Karp & Yoels, 1976). Digital learning breaks through the constraints of space and time imposed by the physical classroom. Online, you can explore insights for as long as it takes—an hour, a day, a week—conducting courses in *unbounded time*, an essential feature required of reflection.

Nearly 100 years ago, American philosopher, psychologist and education reformer John Dewey recognized that reflective thought is nourished by "doubt, hesitation, perplexity" (Dewey, 1930)—frames of mind often discouraged, when certainty, confidence and conviction are demanded of students. "Reflective thinking," Dewey observed. "is always more or less troublesome because it involves overcoming the inertia that inclines one to accept suggestions at their face value; it involves a willingness to endure a condition of mental unrest and disturbance. Reflective thinking, in short, means judgment suspended during further inquiry." Dewey concluded, "Time is required in order to digest impressions and translate them into substantial ideas."

Note

1   Introduced in the late nineteenth and early twentieth century, the Carnegie unit awards academic credit on how much time students spend with classroom instructors. It is defined as 120 hours of contact time with a teacher—an hour of instruction a day, five days a week, for 24 weeks, or 7,200 minutes of instructional time over an academic year (Gaumnitz, 1954).

References

Caspi, A., Chajut, E., Saporta, K. & Beyth-Marom, R. (2006). The influence of personality on social participation in learning environments. *Learning and Individual Differences*, *16*(2), 129–144.

Collins, M. (2013, October 2). *The ideology of anonymity and pseudanonymity. The Huffington Post*. Retrieved from www.huffingtonpost.com/malcolm-collins/online-anonymity_b_3695851.html.

DeCew, J. (2015, Spring). *The Stanford Encyclopedia of Philosophy*. Ed. by E. N. Zalta. Retrieved from http://plato.stanford.edu/archives/spr2015/entries/privacy.

Dewey, J. (1930). *How we think*. Boston, MA: DC Heath.

Fayard, A.-L., & Metiu, A. (2013). *The power of writing in organizations*. New York: Routledge.

Fleming, B. (2014, April 1). *Adaptive learning technology: What it is, why it matters*. Retrieved from www.eduventures.com/2014/04/adaptive-learning-technology-matters/.

Gerstein, R. S. (October 1978). Intimacy and privacy. *Ethics, 89*(1), 76–81.

Grush, M. (December 14, 2011). Monitoring the PACE of student learning: Analytics at Rio Salado College. *Campus Technology.*

Haynie, D. (April 11, 2014). *Minority students should weigh pros, cons of online education.* Retrieved from www.usnews.com/education/online-education/articles/2014/04/11/minority-students-should-weigh-the-pros-and-cons-of-online-education.

Karp, D. A., & Yoels, W. C. (July 1976). The college classroom: Some observations on the meanings of student participation. *Sociology & Social Research, 60*(4), 421–439.

Kassop, M. (May/June 2003). *Ten ways online education matches, or surpasses, face-to-face learning.* Retrieved from The Technology Source Archive website: http://ts.mivu.org/default.asp?show=article&id=1034.

Lapidot-Lefle, A. B. N. (2015). The benign online disinhibition effect: Could situational factors induce self-disclosure and prosocial behaviors? *Cyberpsychology, 9*(2), Article 1.

Levine, A. (October 15, 2015). Let's bid farewell to the Carnegie unit. *Inside Higher Education.*

Marie, B., Feng, M., & Means, B. (2012). *Enhancing teaching and learning through educational data mining and learning analytics.* Washington, DC: US Department of Education.

Nissenbaum, H. (1999). The meaning of anonymity in an information age. *The Information Society, 15*(2), 141–144.

Picciano, A. (2012). The evolution of big data and learning analytics in American higher education. *Journal of Asynchronous Learning Networks, 16*(3), 9–20.

Reflective Thinking. (2015). Wikiversity. Retrieved from https://en.wikiversity.org/wiki/Reflective_thinking.

Semenza, G. (December 11, 2015). Online teaching, it turns out, isn't impersonal. *The Chronicle of Higher Education.*

Suler, J. (July 28, 2004). The online disinhibition effect. *Cyberpsychology and Behavior, 7*(3), 321–326.

Vivolo, J. (2014). Pocket data analytics. In E. R. Richards (Ed.), *ICAS 2014-International conference on analytics driven solutions* (pp. 102–110). Ottawa: Telfer School of Management.

Young, J. R. (January 4, 2016). This chart shows the promise and limits of 'learning analytics'. *The Chronicle of Higher Education.*

5

WHY FACULTY DON'T WANT TO TEACH ONLINE

Like the telephone and the automobile before it, computers have emerged as yet another stubborn technology, we must either master or let life pass us by. But unless you teach at an entirely online school, virtual instruction is not among new inventions you are forced to embrace to live a productive life. At most institutions, faculty have a choice. You may either accommodate yourself to digital education—or safely ignore it. With only a third of college students in the US taking online courses (Allen & Seaman, 2013), most faculty can comfortably let online learning carry on without them, continuing to teach on campus as if nothing has changed.

On-Campus Classrooms

When virtual education is measured against conventional classrooms, the unexamined assumption of most faculty is that the schoolroom is unquestionably superior. Online must prove itself against traditional education. Measuring one against the other, investigators often seek to determine not what is best, but whether virtual education has any worth, and if so, how good is it when compared with the clear superiority of traditional instruction. At the very start, the equation is asymmetrical, with online forced to stand-up against the nearly universal acceptance of the schoolroom as the norm. Rarely does anyone ask, "Is the classroom any good?" But it's the first question raised about digital education. The claims made by those who believe that the traditional classroom is the only proper place for teaching and learning are hardly ever supported by evidence. For most, its superiority over digital and other forms of education is entirely self-evident. There is no need to marshal data to defend it, since it represents the gold standard, the only legitimate space for learning. For many faculty, online education is not only a poor substitute, but an interloper with little to recommend it.

For those who have delivered lectures most of their careers, the intrusion of digital education is often an unwelcome irritation. Largely comfortable with classroom teaching, most faculty are unwilling to step away to sit alone at a computer. For high-status, tenured faculty, there is no better reward than the adulation of students and the emotionally gratifying pleasure professors receive. Why would anyone give it up? In a study of barriers to teaching online, Zane Berge concludes, "Hardly a person exists who eagerly gives up familiar ways of behaving to attempt something that is unknown and is likely to have many serious challenges of implementation" (Berge, 1998). Most faculty go about their academic business paying no attention at all to digital learning.

Many believe that digital intervention in the classroom is wrong-headed, that their lectures are not only supported by centuries of practice, but it's the right thing to do. Giving up physical presence, with its personal engagement and emotional gratification for the quixotic opportunity to teach to an audience you cannot see, seems an entirely foreign, unrewarding exercise, a foolish technological obsession, undoubtedly doomed to fail, following the checkered history of other technological "advances"—film strips, overhead projections, slide carousels, educational TV—that have fallen into ridiculed obsolescence. In his widely admired book, *Being Digital* (Negroponte, 1996), Founding Director of MIT's Media Lab Nicholas Negroponte wonders ". . . how can you possibly hold a conversation with people if you don't know whether they are there? You can't see them, and you don't know how many there are. Are they smiling? Are they even paying attention?"

It's completely understandable why most instructors do not welcome digital learning. With years of practice, faculty know exactly what do to do, precisely what is expected of them, and what they will ask of their students. There is enormous comfort in teaching the way you were taught in grade school, remembering your eager student days when you sat in class in college. Some faculty are so strongly tied to their conduct as teachers, that their professional lives and identity emerge almost entirely from their position in the classroom. After all, what is a professor if she is not lecturing? Blindfolded, a teacher can enter nearly any class, unchanged for centuries, where she can easily finds her way. While many schools have added peripheral devices, such as projectors and smart boards, on the whole, nothing has changed since Victorian times when classrooms and factories were built with pretty much the same purpose—for a docile workforce.

The culture of the classroom is so embedded in our consciousness that its very particular spacial relations and behaviors go largely unexamined. As an instructor, you enter your classroom, and without a second thought, you immediately proceed to your desk up front. As a student, without hesitation, you take your seat in a row, facing the teacher. The physical configuration, position assumed by faculty and students, the conduct of the class, the lecture, student response, duration of classes, length of semesters, credits earned—these and other indelible academic structures and modes of conduct appear as natural as slipping on your socks or tying your laces in the morning. Because it is set in particular space and at discrete times, the physical classroom has established norms that appear self-evident, long established as standard practices, largely based on the received classroom wisdom. Who speaks first? Who permits you to speak? What posture do you assume? Knowing your precise place in this geography can be a great relief for many who worry about their performance in the classroom.

The physical space of the schoolroom mirrors the hierarchy imposed on all of us. Up front, a solid desk signals the position of power, the instructor behind it, facing rows of less solid, less secure desks and seats assigned to students. Power is expressed by the location or symbolic classroom furniture—raised stage, lectern, leather arm chair, massive desk. For some, rather than a place of comfortable engagement, the classroom is a source of anxiety (McKeachie, 1951). Studies reveal that not everyone is happy. Junior faculty, especially women and minorities, suffer severe stress from being judged by different standards (Novek, 1999).

Online instruction overturns nearly everything faculty have learned to depend on. Spacial and architectural configurations disappear. Common positions assumed by faculty and students evaporate. You can no longer exploit your body language, practiced for years—glances, tone of voice, turn of your head, smiles, even stern rebukes. As in a game of pick-up sticks, all normative structures and behaviors you rely on to support your authority fall away. All the props of conventional teaching that comprise the very foundation of what we have come to know as instruction—the classroom itself, your physical presence, even your students—vanish.

Faculty with no online experience often imagine the virtual classroom in unflattering ways—isolated students at home, alienated from their classmates and instructors, engaged in lifeless encounters, mediated by unresponsive screens. Lost in a tangle of inert options, students are estranged from their peers, their teachers, and worst of all, from their studies. For many, online seems an anxious, unsettling placeless place where faculty and students are disoriented.

Face-to-Face and Facebook

Most instructors assume that eye contact in face-to-face instruction gives them enormous confidence that their lectures are being absorbed by their students. Professors say that looking students in the eye is among the most rewarding and certain aspects of instruction. Eyes light up, heads nod. When students lean forward, you sense you are getting through. But does the emotional charge faculty experience actually tell us anything about what students are learning? While there may be enormous emotional gratification from perceived face-to-face engagement, how certain are instructors that the minds of their students are fully present? How many, appearing absorbed, escape the professor's gaze?

We all know from our own experience that a teacher's conviction can be illusory. I remember my own acts of deception as a student when I appeared to display heightened attention to disguise that my mind was actually far away. Pretending to be attentive is common in conversation, you may seem to be participating, but your thoughts have strayed. Musing on things unconnected with what's being said, you may feign interest, but your attention is elsewhere. Often students draw elaborate doodles, pretending to take notes. Emotional and physical discomfort may force some into severe disengagement. Headaches, stomach pain, disappointments in love, at work, may be so intense that they interfere entirely with what's going on.

Today, students can retreat even further. Laptops, smartphones, tablets, and other devices draw attention away to e-mail, texting, social media, and searching, among other electronic distractions. "Resisting the urge to pull out your phone in class is quite difficult for many students . . .. There are texts to answer, e-mails to read, snapchats to send, and rude comments to post on Yik Yak" (Fabris, 2015). In large lecture halls, digital competition is even more appealing, especially when the instructor is not at his best. Faculty who deliver disjointed lectures in a dry, flat, monotonous voice or in an indecipherable accent, invite students to reach out to their friends on Facebook. In a poll conducted by *The Chronicle of Higher Education* (Thomson, 2014), faculty reported on their most-hated classroom distractions, with cell phones rated as worst. One complained that students "are willing to risk failing in class and being publicly rejected in order to check them." In another study (Kolowich, 2015), researchers found, as expected, that freshmen who spent a great deal of time on Facebook, chatting, viewing videos, posting and tagging photos, tended to get poorer grades than others who resist the Internet. MIT scholar Sherry Turkle reports that her students feel "constant connection as a necessity" (Turkle, 2015). "For some, three minutes was too long to go without checking their phones."

Social scientist Erving Goffman, who studied face-to-face interactions in social situations in the 1950s, noted that people can display false attention by controlling their facial muscles so that they appear alert. "We have party faces, funeral faces, and various kinds of institutional faces . . ." (Goffman, 1963). He recognized that while people may appear engaged, they can hide behind what he called "involvement shields," safely disengaged with side activities most instructors censure, like doodling or texting.

"The disciplined ordering of a personal front is one way in which the individual is obliged to express his aliveness to those about him," Goffman observed. While classroom behavior may seem at first to be easily deciphered, reading student engagement is not always transparent. With smiles, nods, and other signs, students can disguise their boredom, hostility, frustration, and other feelings that may betray that they are not actually receiving messages faculty send.

Goffman reminds us that we all have the capacity to divide our attention. We can focus on both principal and side involvements at the same time. "Whether momentary or continuous, simple or complicated, these side activities appear to constitute a fugue-like dissociation of minor muscular activity from the main line of an individual's action."

In class, eagerness, attention, and alertness are often taken as signs that students are absorbing the lesson, but Goffman says that these behaviors are often merely performances, encouraged by academic culture to elicit certain approved responses, leading students to achieve faculty and peer acceptance by exhibiting disciplined conformity. While professors may believe that their students are actually learning what's being taught in class, students may just be performing according to conventional classroom rules.

In an earlier essay (see Chapter 1), I commented on the classroom experience:

> Because students are visible at their desks—rather than invisible in a virtual classroom—somehow we assume that we can know them and understand them. We believe that when we see students in physical space, we can actually gain access to them. Yet it's their invisible qualities that mostly determine who they are. According to [French theorist] Pierre Bourdieu, we forget that the truth of any interaction is never captured entirely by observation. So while face-to-face interaction is often thought of as giving us perfect knowledge of student behavior, in fact, physical presence can often obscure crucially hidden social and psychological relations. We tend to believe that visual cues—facial expressions and body language—offer us sufficient social communication markers to understand one another. Yet these actions, while open to inspection, fail to give us access to unseen psychological and status relationships to which we are often blind. The classroom resists distinctions that are formed by groups and hierarchies that crisscross it from outside. What is visible can often be damaging, turning common experience against us. Hair style, clothes, our perceived ideas of physical beauty, and other personal characteristics can often undermine us, even as they have the capacity to move us closer together. The classroom is a place where ordinary misperceptions by teachers and students can easily defeat effective learning. It is a place where ethnicity, gender, and race are in plain sight, sadly subject to the same stereotypes and prejudices found in the streets.

Goffman adds, "One of the most evident means by which the individual shows himself to be situationally present is through the disciplined management of personal appearance or 'personal front,' that is, the complex of clothing, make-up, hairdo, and other surface decorations he carries about his person."

While it's widely reported that student attention drifts away from the lecturer every seven minutes or so, with some saying that students pay attention for longer periods, say, 10 to 20 minutes, there is very little solid evidence to confirm either claim. Even though it is often cited, the origin of the seven-minute attention span may be found in the depths of the literature; but I confess I was unable to find confident data that supports it. Some research suggests that student concentration decays at about the same rate as workers operating automated equipment, "with serious implications for learning and performance" (Young, 2009). One recent substantive study (Bunce, Flens, & Neils, 2010), however, reports that ". . . attention alternates between being engaged and nonengaged in ever-shortening cycles throughout a lecture segment." Bunce and her colleagues say that while the pattern may vary, depending on how stimulating the instructor and how fascinating the subject, for some, attention may fall away in as little as 30 seconds. The next lapse may occur in about 4.5 minutes and then in shorter and shorter cycles. As expected, and as is almost universally acknowledged, Bunce and her colleagues conclude, ". . . students do not pay attention continuously during a 50-minute lecture."

With the conventional lecture under siege for years, it's mystifying why so many faculty place so much confidence in it. Since the nineteenth and early twentieth century, radical educators have not only expressed serious doubt about its value, but have vigorously campaigned to dislodge it from its central place in education. John Dewey, Paolo Freire, Lev Vigotsky, and other champions of active learning, recognized years ago that deep-rooted learning doesn't happen in classrooms where students passively listen to lectures (see Chapter 1). "The sage-on-a-stage model of instruction has dominated higher education since the Middle Ages," reports Ryan Craig in *Wired*. "Today, surveys of faculty members reveal that 70 to 90 percent of classroom time is spent 'transferring information' via lecture" (Craig, 2014).

Noted online scholar Eric Fredericksen remarks that faculty tend to "romanticize the traditional classroom" (Fredericksen, 2015), observing that while thoughtful, small seminars can be enormously gratifying and pedagogically stimulating, they are far from standard classroom experience. At most US universities, students do not participate in small, intimate engagements, but on the contrary, in large enrollment courses, where a few hundred—or even several hundred—attend lectures in giant auditoriums. "There is virtually no interaction between student and instructor or students with their classmates," Fredericksen concludes.

What is especially confounding is that in nearly every other part of their lives, faculty engage, like the rest of us, in virtual worlds. With the nearly universal penetration of the Internet into everyone's life, it's a rare electronic hermit who escapes e-mailing, social media, texting, shopping online or streaming favorite shows on Apple TV. In their professional lives, scholars routinely depend on the Internet, with nearly all periodicals, not only easily accessible online, but often entirely out of reach in print in university libraries. It is practically impossible today to perform advanced research without searching the Web, accessing databases, or specialized software. The Web is at the center of modern scholarly communications. You cannot submit an article for publication or attend a conference in your field without entering your data on a screen. Every stage of your research is facilitated by information technology, with your data stored in the cloud. Together with data mining, visualization and other techniques, your results are extended globally (Borgman, 2007).

The most recent blow aimed at unseating the dominance of classroom lectures comes from a new meta-analysis, the largest and most comprehensive study of its kind, published in the prestigious *Proceedings of the National Academy of Sciences (PNAS)*. Comparing standard lectures with active learning in undergraduate science and math classes in more than 200 studies, the outcome came as no surprise to educators who had long suspected that the lecture's dominance was coming to an end. Results showed that the "average test scores improved by about six percent in active learning sections, and that students in classes with traditional lectures were 1.5 times more likely to fail than were students in classes with active learning" (Scott Freeman, 2014). Interviewed by *Wired*, Scott Freeman, the principal author of the *PNAS* review, called attention to a critical conclusion. "There is a *growing body of evidence* showing that active learning differentially benefits students of color and/or students from disadvantaged backgrounds and/or women in male-dominated fields," he said. "It's not a stretch to claim that lecturing actively discriminates against underrepresented students (Bhatia, 2014)." In a startling observation, when star faculty lectures were matched against inexperienced active learning instructors, students still performed better in active classes. "We've yet to see any evidence that celebrated lecturers can help students more than even first-generation active learning does," Freeman concluded. In an article in *Forbes*, Tim Zimmer of the University of Pennsylvania says, "The pedagogical view that instruction must be taught in the traditional classroom has long been defeated" (Zimmer, 2014).

Status

Teaching online can be a dangerous career move, departing from the comfortable respectability of conventional classrooms for the exotic, suspicious digital world. Senior faculty, protected under a crown of scholarly achievement, can take chances. They can go online with only modest concern that their reputations are at stake. But junior faculty without tenure face potentially serious consequences. Online instruction can be a foolish step, seen by your peers as risky, departing from conventional academic practice. In the hierarchy of status, if you teach online, do you compromise your position?

Faculty who are thinking of teaching online must confront a series of professional and personal conflicts. What will her peers think of her? Will she be devalued, suspect, even ridiculed? Will her career be threatened? Will her colleagues say that her choice is foolish? Will she be exposed to hostile reactions from her colleagues? Will spending time teaching online prevent her from engaging in research? Or will she be seen by some as adventurous, a risk-taker, an early adapter, unafraid of challenges? If you teach online, your commitment to scholarship may be questioned. Why did you go online when your future depends on publishing results of your research, not engaging in virtual instruction? At some schools, academic departments strongly discourage young faculty from teaching online. It's considered a distraction from your career objectives, while teaching on campus is not only part of your commitment to a full professional life, but required for most junior faculty as their first step in climbing the academic hierarchy. While teaching is part of what propels your career—especially if glowing student evaluations raise your profile—at most universities, the quality and productivity of your research plays the most decisive role in keeping you on track to earn promotion and secure tenure. Quality on-campus teaching may contribute to your rise in the ranks—but, rarely, if ever, does online instruction. At nearly all schools, online is almost never mentioned in academic rules that judge faculty. If you teach online, you may do it for extra compensation—called "overload," paid above your basic salary—or for the personal satisfaction of participating in what some believe is the next stage in the evolution of higher education. But teaching online may not be a wise move to further your academic career.

The historic conservatism of faculty, jealous of its prestige, tends to guard its entrenched culture (Mintzberg, 1979). To some, online learning represents a threat that must be challenged and arrested. Troubled by the vulgar encroachment of technology into the classroom, hostile faculty battle digital education. "I'm concerned about the academic integrity in all online classes," commented one faculty member in response to a survey. "Especially in classes where the instructor may never see the students." In their desire to preserve the past, nostalgic faculty often conflate digital education with the deterioration of standards, declining faculty authority, even the danger posed by radical politics. The desire to return to an earlier, purer past, unpolluted by technology and other irritating intrusions, gives faculty a license to attack virtual education as yet another encroachment on their former independence. Some faculty long to retreat to simpler times, untangled in a web of digital mischief. Online learning is yet another offensive burden faculty are asked to shoulder, along with student evaluations, course outcomes, assessments, research impact factors, citation ranking, and other data-driven obsessions imposed by university bureaucracy, accreditors, and the state. According to Svetlana Boym, in her insightful book, *The Future of Nostalgia* (Boym, 2001), nostalgia "is a yearning for a different time—the time of our childhood, the slower rhythms of our dreams. In a broader sense, nostalgia is rebellion against the modern idea of time, the time of history and progress . . . a longing for continuity, social cohesion and tradition." German philosopher and critic Walter Benjamin (Benjamin, 2008), referring not to university courses, but to works of art, suggested in the 1930s that the intervention of technology undermines the halo of old values. Technology, Benjamin claimed, unsettles the weight derived from tradition. According to Benjamin, what distinguishes traditional art from technologically reproduced works is their "aura." With the introduction of digital means of delivery, the great scholar, declaiming at the lectern, may no longer hold us spellbound. Recently, MOOCs (Massive Open-source Online Courses), unwittingly revealed the effect of technology as it peels away academic glamor from notable MIT, Harvard and Stanford faculty who videostream their lectures to tens of thousands online. Rather than being glued to their seats, fewer than ten percent enrolled in MOOCs actually hold out to the very end (Jordan, 2014). Many escape minutes into the very first lesson.

What Do They Say?

In a survey conducted by my colleague John Vivolo (Vivolo, 2014) about why some faculty are reluctant to teach online, more than half of the NYU Tandon School of Engineering faculty surveyed believe that virtual instructors have no personal relationship with their students. They also think teaching online offers little interaction with students and that there is little student-to-student engagement. They concluded that, on the whole, online quality is not as good as on campus. Most studies of faculty attitudes confirm these findings, especially the belief that online content is inferior. A comprehensive literature survey (Lloyd, 2012) concluded that most faculty have strong reservations about online teaching, believing that because virtual instructors do not exchange visual cues with students, digital education is not nearly as effective. Lloyd's study uncovers the troubling fact that faculty with the deepest resistance are those with the least familiarity with digital instruction. Conversely, the more faculty know about it, the less they reject it. The study concluded that "faculty with the least experience with online education perceived the barriers as greater than those who had the most experience," revealing that faculty who know the least are those who express the strongest opposition. Since most faculty have little or no experience with virtual education, resistance is widespread. Not surprisingly, Lloyd's data showed that older and higher ranking faculty exhibit the least tolerance, suggesting that faculty with the greatest authority, those in the most powerful university positions, can exploit their bias by erecting steep barriers to institutional acceptance. It's disheartening to find that at the intellectual heart of our culture, where conventional ideas are subject to serious investigation, where commonplace notions face critical inquiry, faculty opinion about online education emerges with the same carelessness of thought casually offered by any passerby outside the campus gates. In their resistance to virtual instruction, faculty can disregard their highest intellectual aims—openness to new ideas, exploration of unexpected possibilities, curiosity. British social theorist Jacqueline Rose remarks ". . . there is no limit to what people will do to hold on to their belief in themselves" (Rose, 2013).

In a number of studies, faculty express serious concerns about the lack of institutional commitment, chief among them is poor technical and pedagogical support, sending novice instructors, unprepared to navigate unchartered digital space. At some schools, with little or no support, faculty are given an access code to their online class and sent into virtual space entirely without preparation—sink or swim. While university instructors have been sent into on-campus classrooms for centuries without pedagogical instruction, online, the consequences can be serious. Virtual faculty also say they are inadequately compensated for the time it takes to migrate courses from on-campus classrooms. They also worry about institutional ownership of their intellectual property. Historically, faculty own the rights to their scholarship, with the freedom to write books, publish results, consult, and do whatever they please with their work, even picking up a course they delivered at one university and teaching the same content at another school. At most institutions, faculty still maintain the same publishing and other privileges, but commonly they may not take their virtual course developed at one place and take it to another (see Chapter 8).

Teaching on campus is not a team sport. Except in rare cases of team-teaching, faculty enter on-campus classrooms entirely on their own. They prepare classes on their own, create syllabi, devise slides, and hand out assignments all by themselves. What they teach and how they teach it is almost entirely in their own hands. What happens in the classroom is completely under their authority. Online, the autonomy of the instructor is threatened. Because digital instruction requires technical and pedagogical support from sophisticated videographers, instructional designers, and other personnel, faculty join as members of a pedagogical team, rather than as autonomous instructors. Anything might happen. Online courses, inhabited by ghostly students, may even appear dangerous, potentially mutinous, undermining academic discipline. It's no wonder faculty fear losing control. In a national survey, noted investigators Elaine Allen and Jeff Seaman found that, over all, (Seaman, 2012) faculty are fairly pessimistic about digital instruction, with those at institutions with no online courses, overwhelmingly concluding that virtual education is "inferior" or "somewhat inferior" to face-to-face teaching. While more positive, even online instructors have doubts, with about half saying they are concerned about the quality of digital courses.

Disruption

Dogged by falling enrollments, rising tuition, and unsupportable student debt, universities are under pressure to find new ways to dig themselves out of their economic troubles. For many schools, online education looks like a good candidate to reverse these intractable trends. Trustees and state legislatures imagine that digital learning is not only an agent of change, but offers the potential to lower costs and increase enrollment. For universities with limited resources, digital classes can deliver enormous benefits. Online courses require very little—merely faculty and students in virtual space. Other than compensating online instructors and installing technical infrastructure, nearly all other expenses—apart from websites, recruitment, and managing student applications and acceptance—fall away. Online, vast investments in classrooms, lecture halls, laboratories, cafeterias, dormitories, sports facilities, plus ancillary expenses required to operate and maintain a modern campus—food services, security, parking, grounds—bricks and mortar disappear in cyberspace. Compared with the enormous sums needed to run a giant university campus, launching classes online is trivial. By jumping on the "creative disruption" (Christensen & Eyring, 2011) bandwagon, colleges hope that online learning will stop run-away costs. Unless schools adopt digital instruction, noted Harvard scholar Clayton Christensen claims, higher education is at risk. In his Darwinian narrative, only those who adapt will survive. But it's unlikely that technological intervention will reverse the economic plight of the nation's universities. The causes are far more structural, with the withdrawal of state funding from public institutions, the introduction of costly non-academic bureaucracies, the increasingly demanding load of financing complex campuses, and the long-term shift of the financial burden on student families.

As schools move ahead more aggressively introducing online programs, the demand for digital instructors rises in parallel. Decades ago, at the dawn of Web-based education, only those who felt that online learning represented a major advance in teaching and learning signed on. Early adopters were drawn to it for its promise of learner-centered education, encouraging peer-to-peer student participation and teamwork, styles of education championed by progressive educators. With the expansion of new online programs, universities must populate digital courses with reluctant faculty, instructors who are not drawn to virtual education intuitively for its innovative pedagogy, but who often doubt its value. At many schools, professors are under pressure to adapt, to acquiesce to university demands to teach online. When online instruction becomes a requirement, those who oppose it can emerge as defenders of academic virtue, justifying their resistance by claiming that online is damaging the university by disseminating poor quality goods.

In a survey of faculty attitudes to digital demands (Novek, 1999), Eleanor Novek reported that faculty were anxious about the personal economic conse-quences of online learning. "Machines have historically been used to increase profits by cutting the labor force," warned one professor. "Computers in higher education will probably have a similar effect." Another cautioned, "I am very leery of distance learning, since it seems to be suggested in order to solve budget problems." Novek concluded, "As the institutional clamor for technology grows louder around them, some individual faculty members are making connections between downsizing of the economy, the push to computerize, and their own previously secure employment. Academics are beginning to ask the same kinds of questions that workers in other professions have been asking for quite awhile . . . . Will computers wind up eliminating our jobs and devaluing our research? In short, are we, too, about to made obsolete?"

The trend to eliminate full-time, tenure-track faculty, and replace them with adjuncts and other part-time instructors began long before universities introduced digital courses. As states squeeze public universities by withdrawing government funds from higher education, colleges must stretch shrinking budgets to accommodate student enrollment. Turning to a legion of lower-paid adjuncts looks like an easy way out. According to national survey (Association of Governing Boards of Universities and Colleges, 2013), the percentage of permanent, full-time positions at the nation's universities fell from 78 percent in 1969 to 33 percent today. Because virtual courses can be delivered easily from anywhere at any time, a contingent adjunct army, prepared to drop everything to teach online as demand rises, emerges as an attractive feeder for a hungry virtual education market (Bedford, 2000). Adjuncts are the itinerant academic working class, struggling to find employment at any price, willing to teach at three or four schools to make ends meet. On average, adjunct faculty earn merely a third of full-time faculty at the nation's universities (Curtis & Thornton, 2013).

For-profit universities depend almost exclusively on a contingent academic workforce. For years, for-profits dominated online industry, with hundreds of thousands of students attending schools like the Universities of Phoenix, Capella, and Corinthian, until the federal government stepped in (Ruch, 2001). Owing to recent stricter regulations, a number of for-profits shed half their students in less than a year. Some, like Corinthian, filed for bankruptcy, closing dozens of campuses. While for-profits may have played a positive social role at first by offering college education to low-income, first-generation students, greed undermined them, turning them into diploma mills, absorbing billions of dollars in wasted federal student loans. At best, only half of the students enrolled in for-profits graduate (Blumenstyk, 2012). Because for-profits were among the first to champion digital education and because they still represent a sizeable segment, faculty at public and private colleges often dismiss digital education, fearing that if their schools embrace it, their institutions will fall into the same contemptible void.

The case against online education is not without merit. When run by for-profits, it can be a scam. In the hands of underfunded and poorly managed public and private institutions, online learning delivers mediocre education at best. If these failures represent the sum of online education, then faculty who reject it have every reason not only to be suspicious, but to discredit it. Why would you walk out of your solid classroom for an academic practice that melts into air? But the university is not monolithic. There are faculty who have concluded that the old ways do not make much sense anymore, that traditional classrooms can no longer be defended academically. For many, the battle is not fought between brick-and-mortar and new digital space, but between old and new ways of teaching—between wise, old talking heads at the blackboard versus new approaches that encourage interaction among students and instructor.

What the Literature Says

Solid research over many years fails to support the overwhelming negative attitudes held by most faculty. Studies that have investigated effectiveness, retention and achievement, by and large conclude that virtual instruction can be as good or better than on campus. (Bernard et al., 2004). A massive US Department of Education review of the literature showed that students taking online classes performed modesty better than their peers studying on campus. The report found that, "On average, students in online learning conditions performed better than those receiving face-to-face instruction" (Means, 2009).

Results of online graduate programs at NYU Tandon School of Engineering (Newswire, 2015) confirm the clear benefits of virtual education. Online student data at the school often show superior outcomes when compared with the nation's science and engineering on-campus Master's students, with 96 percent of the school's online students completing their online courses and 89 percent of the school's online Master's students earning their graduate degrees in three years. Online faculty and students on average spend about 15 hours per week in their virtual courses. As is common, when comparing grades in online with on-campus classes, they are startlingly the same, semester after semester.

If you go online, the effort to re-think how you will present your content and re-assemble your syllabus, requires serious commitment, especially if you must now become a student yourself to learn how to be proficient at navigating software, a skill that requires you to be adept at things that may come more naturally to your students. "Migrating a course from lecture to active learning format is as much work as developing a brand new course," notes Ryan Craig in *Wired* (Craig, 2014). Going online is like moving to a foreign country, where you must learn a new language and assimilate a new culture. Most of us might conclude that online education merely requires that schools replicate the physical classroom in digital space. It turns out, however, that online learning is not simply the result of introducing technical means to migrate the campus experience online. Online technology demands far greater instructional insights than are found on campus.

Observers often wonder what it takes to be a good virtual instructor. In my experience, the best on-campus faculty are best online, too. Devoted to their students and committed to student success, they give serious thought to devising compelling ways to teach, online or on-campus. To be an exemplary teacher—in virtual or physical space—you must enter the minds of your students, recognizing the struggle each confronts, remembering your own trials as a student. Online faculty must be as generous with their students under their care as those on campus. They must enter the virtual classroom sympathetically, recognizing that virtual space requires faculty to be accommodating with remote students who may find the online environment alienating at first. Faculty must find innovate ways to engage students they can neither see nor hear. Devoted to their students, the best teachers commonly love what they do and often love their students, eager to do what's best for them; no different online than on campus. Cynical teachers who disparage their students are not cut out for it, whether they teach virtually or on campus.

As digital education enters the mainstream, more online and on-campus faculty inhabit the same person. Even today, many teachers offer courses in conventional classrooms, and during the same semester, they may deliver the same class in virtual space, with the same content at the same university to residential students in one section and distant learners in another (see Chapter 6). Today, the two practices, virtual and physical, are no longer guarded at checkpoints. Blended, or hybrid, digital learning has infiltrated the university with a bundle of technologies, first introduced online, now almost universally available to on-campus to faculty and residential students. Nearly all schools provide access to learning management systems, not only to remote students, but to everyone. Border crossing occurs so frequently that the division between online and on-campus is rapidly disappearing. Technology has penetrated the classroom so deeply that the distinction will soon be obsolete. At many schools, however, the divide still separates remote from on-campus students. While residential students are privileged with cafés, sports facilities, and bookstores, students at a distance often receive inferior services from school administrators who fail to take the needs of distance students into account. "Just come in to my office," is not a helpful response to remote students who may live thousands of miles from campus.

My own experience reveals the power of miraculous conversion, especially when a noted faculty member, who has dug his heels in against digital learning for years, suddenly embraces it. A number of years ago, at a small technical school in New Jersey, a serious scholar, revered for the depth of his research achievements, who for many years was among the most opposed to virtual education, made an about-face, not merely accepting online instruction grudgingly, he emerged as a champion. Soon after his conversion, faculty resistance at the school began to crumble. Introduction of new converts accelerated, climbing higher and higher, until nearly all faculty became believers. When I first started at the school, just a handful agreed to teach online. Over the next three or four years, a few dozen volunteered. In the end, following the noted faculty's conversion, 90 percent of the faculty were teaching online. The decision to teach online does not come easily. Apart from leaving the comfort of your on-campus classroom, you will face a cascade of complex challenges. You must imagine what it's like to enter a class whose students are invisible. While computers are essential, online learning is not a software product. Unexpectedly, its principal innovations are pedagogical, not technological. From its inception, online was open to inventive practices that challenge conventional teaching —teamwork, project-based, adaptive, and peer-to-peer learning, among other creative pedagogies that encourage active learning (see Chapter 3). To perform successfully, you must know how to exploit a bundle of digital applications— e-mail, learning management systems and multimedia, among other software.

But these are merely mediating components. Not a device, the strengths of online education emerge from new conceptual approaches in teaching and learning. In dismissing it for its dependence on technology, opponents overlook crucial elements that make digital education transformative—an entirely new way of teaching with new methods of engaging students. In the long run, neither the guardians of the campus nor the champions of the digital revolution, will claim victory. Already, the educational battleground is populated by faculty who accept that it is neither physical nor virtual space, but new pedagogical practices that support active student learning that will triumph.

References

Allen, E. I. & Seaman, J. (2013). *Changing course: Ten years of online education in the United States*. Newburyport, MA: Sloan Consortium.

Association of Governing Boards of Universities and Colleges. (2013). *2013 survey on technology and instruction*. Washington, DC: Association of Governing Boards of Colleges and Universities.

Bedford, L. (2000, Fall). The professional adjunct. *Online Journal of Distance Learning Administration*, 7(3).

Benjamin, W. (2008). *The work of art in the age of its technological reproducibility*. Cambridge, MA: Belknap Press of Harvard University Press.

Berge, Z. L. (1998, Summer). Barriers to online teaching in post secondary institutions: Can policy changes fix it? *Online Learning of Distance Learning Administration*, 1(2), 2.

Bernard, R. M., Abrami, P. C., Lou, Y., Borokhovski, E., Wade, A., Wozney, L., Wallet, P. A., Fiset, M., & Huang, B. (2004, Fall). How does distance education compare with classroom instruction? A meta-analysis of the empirical literature. *Review of Educational Research*, 74(3), 379–439.

Bhatia, A. (May 12, 2014). Empirical Zeal. *Wired*.

Blumenstyk, G. (March 2, 2012,). For-profit college compute their own graduation rates. *The Chronicle of Higher Education*.

Borgman, C. (2007). *Scholarship in the digital age*. Cambridge, MA: MIT Press.

Boym, S. (2001). *The future of nostalgia*. New York: Basic Books.

Bunce, D. M., Flens, E. A. & Neiles, K. Y. (October 22, 2010). How long can students pay attention in class? A study of student attention decline using clickers. *Journal of Chemical Education*, 87(12), 1438–1443.

Christensen, C. & Eyring, H. (2011). *The innovative university*. San Francisco, CA: Jossey Bass.

Craig, R. (2014, October 27). Rethinking the lecture in the information age: It's time to flip the classroom. *Wired*.

Curtis, J., & Thornton, S. (March–April 2013). Annual report of the economic status of the profession, 2012–2013. *Academe*.

Fabris, C. (February 2, 2015). App gives students an incentive to keep their phones locked in class. *The Chronicle of Higher Education*.

Fredericksen, E. (November 3, 2015). Private communication.

Freeman Scott, S. E. (June 10, 2014). Active learning increases student performance in science, engineering, and mathematics. *Proceedings of the National Academy of Science*, 111(23), 8410–8415.

Goffman, E. (1963). *Behavior in public places*. New York: The Free Press.

Jordan, K. (2014). Initial trends in enrolment and completion of massive open online courses. *The International Journal of Research in Open and Distributed Learning, 15*(1). 133–160.

Kolowich, S. (January 21, 2015). Facebook addiction. *The Chronicle of Higher Education*.

McKeachie, W. (1951). Anxiety in the college classroom. *The Journal of Education Research, 45*(2), 153–160.

Means, B. E. (2009). Evaluation of evidence-based practices in online learning: A meta analysis and review of online learning studies. Washington, DC: US Department of Education.

Mintzberg, H. (1979). The professional bureaucracy. In M. C. Brown (Ed.), *Organization & Governance in higher education* (5th ed., pp. 50–70). Boston, MA: Pearson.

Negorponte, N. (1996). *Being digital*. New York: Vintage.

Newswire. (October 15, 2015). NYU Tandon school of engineering wins national online learning prize. *The Street*.

Novek, E. M. (1999). Do professors dream of electronic students? Faculty anxiety and the new information technologies. *Eastern Communication Association Annual Meeting*. Charleston, WV.

Rose, J. (2013). *The last resistance*. London: Verso.

Ruch, R. (2001). *Higher ed, inc*. Baltimore, MD: Johns Hopkins University Press.

Seaman, E. A. (2012). *Conflicted: Faculty and online education*. Wellesley, MA: Inside Higher Education.

Thomson, A. (September 4, 2014). Your 3 worst classroom, distractions (and How to Deal with Them). *The Chronicle of Higher Education*.

Turkle, S. (October 2, 2015). How to teach in an age of distraction. *The Chronicle of Higher Education*.

Vivolo, J. (2014). Fighting the tide: Understanding and combating resistance to online learning. *International Conference on Online Learning*. Orlando, FL: Online Learning Consortium.

Young, M. S. (2009). Students pay attention! *Active Learning in Higher Education, 10*(1), 41–55.

Zimmer, T. (October 23, 2014). Rethinking higher ed: A case for adaptive learning. *Forbes*.

6

BLIND SCORES IN A GRADUATE TEST

Conventional Compared with Online Outcomes

With M. Hosein Fallah

While the published literature suggests that there is little or no difference in the outcomes of student results when online learning is compared with conventional classroom instruction[1], an opportunity arose in the spring of 2000 to compare two graduate school environments—one in a conventional setting and other in an online virtual classroom. The two classes were taught by the same instructor who delivered the same content to both groups. In order to eliminate potential instructor bias, either in favor of his online students, or conversely, in favor of his face-to-face (FTF) students, a procedure was devised to permit the instructor to grade mid-term examinations from both classes without the instructor knowing from which class the exams originated. The "blind" study was performed at Stevens Institute of Technology, a technical and business university that provides undergraduate and graduate education to approximately 4,000 students.

In addition to offering graduate certificates in conventional settings, beginning in 2000, Stevens introduced three entirely online courses as part of an initiative to offer certificates to graduate students online. To differentiate its entirely online offerings from those delivered conventionally, the school created an Internet learning environment at its WebCampus Stevens site, www.webcampus.stevens.edu.

WebCampus instructors and students employ the courseware application platform, WebCT, with standard tools for interactivity, study, and other online learning functions. The site also provides access to the school's digital library, bookstore, advising, application forms, tuition payment, enrollment, and other services online. Admittance to the online graduate school is the same as that for conventional study. Requirements, student background, tuition, and other elements are exactly the same for both modes.

The online learning environment grew out of Stevens' earlier and on-going introduction of web-based and other technologically enhanced course delivery. In addition, the school delivers graduate programs to corporate sites via interactive video facilities. Together with WebCampus entirely online delivery, the school will offer more than 100 electronically enhanced distance learning courses in 2001.

Study Background

One of the core courses in the Telecommunications Management graduate program at Stevens is "Regulation and Policy in the Telecommunications Industry." The course provides students with an understanding of the evolution of telecommunications policy in the US, the breakup of the Bell System, Communications Act of 1996, and current issues in deregulation of the industry. Students enroll as part of a requirement for a graduate certificate or Master's degree in Telecommunications Management. Parallel sessions are offered on and off campus each semester.

In early 2000, the school began offering its Telecommunications Management graduate certificate program online. The regulation and policy course was one of the first to be delivered entirely online. Although content remained the same as in the conventional offering, it was redesigned for delivery on the courseware applications platform, WebCT. The online course was offered in parallel with conventional sessions.

At mid-term, we decided to compare the effect of digital learning with conventional education. Even though there has been a good deal of research comparing the effectiveness of online teaching with that of conventional in-class lectures, this study introduced a "blind" test, making it unique.

These are the elements contained in the research environment:

1. **Course Content.** Course content, textbook used[2], reading and homework assignments, and quizzes were the same for both classes.
2. **Instruction.** The instructor was the same in both classes.
3. **Examination.** The mid-term examination given to students in both groups was the same.
4. **Venue and Proctoring.** Both online and on-campus students were required to come to campus for their mid-term exam. Online students had not seen each other or their instructor prior to the day of the test. A teaching assistant proctored the test for both groups.
5. **Blind Study Procedure.** The proctor shuffled the test papers, so that they were completely intermingled. A number was assigned to each test, and the student names were removed. Following the procedure, the tests were given to the instructor for grading. After grading, the student names were matched to the tests to record the results.

Findings

The test results for each group are shown in Figure 6.1. The virtual class had seven students whose test grades ranged from 57 to 94 (out of 100 points). The on–campus class, with 12 students, received mid–term grades ranging from 35 to 87.

From a quick inspection of the raw data, it is not immediately clear which class did better. The distribution of the grades in Figure 6.2, however, shows that while the means of two samples are close, the on–campus class has a bi–modal

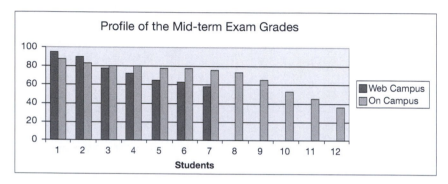

Figure 6.1 Profile of Mid-term Exam Grades

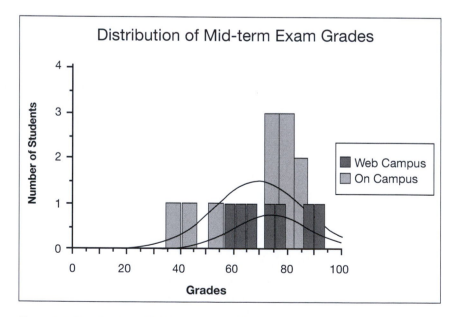

Figure 6.2 Distribution of Mid-term Exam Grades

Table 6.1 Statistical Comparison of Data from Mid-term Exams

	WebCampus	On-campus
No. of students	7	12
Mean	74.0	68.7
Std. Deviation	13.9	16.5
Two-tailed t-test	0.025, 17 = -0.71	P = 0.49 n.s.

distribution, with some students scoring high and some low. We will discuss this difference in our observation.

We then took a closer look by examining the statistics. This data is shown in Table 6.1. The average score for the online class was five points (five percent) higher than for the on-campus class. The online class scores also had less variation. The standard deviation for the online class was 13.9, compared to 16.5 for the on-campus class. To see if the difference in the means is significant, given the small sample size, we used a "t" test. The null hypothesis (the means are equal) could not be rejected.

While the study closely follows many results reported in the literature, a number of observations about the student population in this study are important:

1. *Independent Learning.* We believe that online learning placed greater pressure on students to perform in dependent learning.
2. *Student Retention.* The number of dropouts from the online class was greater than in the conventional class (five vs. two). We believe that students who could not meet the demands of their online class dropped out after a few weeks, leaving a more homogeneous group in the class. This observation is supported by a tighter distribution of grades for this group and its smaller standard deviation.
3. *Student Population.* Even though students self-selected their enrollment in the classes offered, all students enrolled in the online class were working professionals. Those enrolled in the conventional class were full-time students and working professionals.
4. *Student Personality Characteristics.* The students who continued in the online class are more mature personally and professionally, some holding managerial positions in their companies.

While this "blind" study confirms the results from previous research, showing largely that there is little or no difference in student outcomes when online learning is compared with on-campus classroom experiences, the investigators believe that other factors may be significant; namely, it may take greater student maturity to sustain a commitment to self-motivated study in an online environment.

Notes

1   Russell, Thomas E. (2001). *The no significant difference phenomenon* (5th ed.). IDECC. Retrieved from http://nosignificantdifference.org/.
2   Brock, Gerald W. (1998). *Telecommunication policy for the information age: From monopoly to competition*. Harvard University Press.

This article was originally published as "Blind Scores in a Graduate Test: Conventional Compared with Web-based Outcomes," co-authored with M. Hosein Fallah, in the Journal of Asynchronous Learning Networks (JALN), *Vol. 4, No. 2, December 2000.*

PART II
Migrating Online

7

MIGRATING ONLINE

With Frank Mayadas

As the online learning train picks up speed across the academic landscape, hundreds of colleges and universities have come on board[1]—some with merely a handful of students, others with tens of thousands. At institutions that have yet to climb on, many wonder whether it's worth creating potential conflicts with faculty, staff, and trustees. Is it worth carrying the burden of a new infrastructure? What are the academic consequences? On what basis is online education justified? Colleges and universities offer online programs for many cogent reasons—some having to do with the institution's mission, others for prudent economic motives, and still others for a variety of other aims. Most offer virtual education to achieve intertwined goals. As Table 7.1 shows, online learning gives schools the opportunities to explore various strategic objectives with a number of implications.

Learning Effectiveness[2]

When most people think of online learning, the image that frequently comes to mind is of an isolated student facing a computer screen, entirely alone. Although this perception is partly correct—digital learning is performed by an individual stationed at a screen—the fact is that most digital courses at colleges and universities in the United States are actually highly interpersonal, instructor-led, and take place in a "virtual classroom," with other classmates participating continuously in "threaded discussions" and in other interactive activities over the Internet. For many, the online experience can be far less alienating than in a conventional classroom. Over the last decade, numerous scholarly efforts have sought to determine the efficacy of online education. Most of the literature compares traditional classroom delivery with technology-supported education. By now—even though conventional wisdom holds that the campus constitutes

Table 7.1 Institutional Objectives in Online Learning Strategies

Institutional objectives indicated below are matched in the right-hand columns by strategic areas with which they most closely align	Social	Research	Pedagogy	Economic
Extend mission outside region, beyond conventional constituency	•	•	•	•
Provide flexible teaching and learning locations and schedules	•	•	•	•
Give access to students who cannot attend class on-campus	•	•		•
Extend the democratization of the university	•			
Secure additional revenue				•
Supplement in-class lectures			•	
Perform research on alternative learning and instruction methods		•	•	
Introduce innovative teaching and learning practices		•	•	
Provide new programs without new classrooms, facilities			•	•
Give students the experience of working with online tools		•	•	
Provide extended opportunities to learn collaboratively	•	•	•	
Allow interaction with other parts of the country, other cultures	•	•	•	
Extend the learning space from the classroom to the world	•	•	•	

the *sine qua non* of an educational experience—accumulated evidence from thousands of studies shows that there is "no significant difference" between the two modes.[3] One of the supporting "pillars" of the Online Learning Consortium (OLC), the leading professional organization of institutions committed to quality online education (http://onlinelearningconsortium.org/), is the assurance that schools offer the same quality online as they do in traditional programs. According to this principle, "interaction is the key"—with online courses encouraging interaction of students with their instructors, classmates, and materials almost daily.

At institutions currently engaged in—or considering—delivering online courses, schools must collect quantifiable data to establish baseline results. These must be measured against continuing efforts to improve or extend digital education. When colleges collect outcomes data from students in conventional classrooms—test scores, grades, and course and program completion rates, among other information—they must gather them equally for remote students. According to OLC guidelines on learning effectiveness, online programs must track instructional methods, student populations, and class size, with each institution aiming to guarantee that the quality of instruction, whether on campus or online, achieves comparable learning outcomes. This key principle not only ensures high student learning standards, but also is critically important for institutional accreditation. Recent objectives issued by the regional higher education accrediting bodies for online as well as on-campus programs depend on institutions securing rich comparative quantitative results that show that both modes offer the same content, with the same—or equally qualified—faculty at the same standard[4].

Most educators agree that the debate over the quality of online learning versus conventional classroom teaching is no longer as contentious as it was when virtual education first entered higher education over two decades ago. Research is turning to more complex questions about the value of online learning. Do certain students—say, for example, foreign born who fear their accents place them at a disadvantage in traditional classrooms—perform better online? Does online learning offer working professionals the opportunity to complete their degrees more rapidly than in conventional settings? Are women—who now make up a far greater proportion of students online than men—more likely to participate actively than in conventional male-dominated classrooms? What about the effectiveness of online learning for black, Hispanic, and other underrepresented students? Are there benefits for physically or psychologically challenged students? This is the next—and far more difficult—phase of quantifying the value of online learning than routine test scores or grades. In the largest and most comprehensive study of online compared with on-campus student performance for the US Department of Education, Barbara Means and her colleagues found that on the whole, virtual students performed better than students in conventional classes[5].

Access

As colleges and universities shift dramatically from housing traditional, full-time residential students to a larger adult and part-time population[6]—students who do not require dormitories or athletic facilities—the demand for remote learning expands in parallel. Eduventures, an educational consulting firm, reports that "non-traditional students—of which working adults compose the vast majority —have been the fastest growing demographic segment" of the higher education student population." These busy, consumer-savvy students are looking for quality, convenience, and flexibility—qualities that align closely with . . . web-based distance learning."[7]

Institutions that have not taken steps to open their gates to adult and part-time learners may have already begun to see their enrollments flatten or decline. Schools offering online educational opportunities openly invite non-traditional students—a population that may be prevented from enrolling in residential colleges or even coming to school at a set time of day or evening because of obligations at work or at home. Because of family or job demands, students at a considerable distance—either in this country or abroad—may not be able to attend classes at a campus far from home, making it impossible for them to enroll in programs that may be especially suited to them. Some may not be able to take courses on campus because of other, even more serious, obstacles. For many, physical, language, social, or psychological barriers turn the classroom into a troubling, rather than a welcoming, environment. Virtual classes commonly meet personal needs. Over numerous surveys, the principal reason given by students as to why they take online classes is *convenience*. Even those located just around the corner from campus often find going online more accessible. Consider those who work fulltime or whose job requires frequent travel. Parents with young children, families with elderly parents or others who need to be cared for at home. OLC, in its guidelines on access, declares, "All learners who wish to learn online have the opportunity and can achieve success."

Marketing and promotion of online courses depends crucially on the audience schools expect to serve. Institutions that plan to deliver online courses essentially to their present population, either to supplement traditional instruction or to shift students from a physical to a virtual classroom, will promote their programs quite differently from those that plan to reach out around the country or around the world. Local recruitment often requires exploiting conventional vehicles—print catalogs, posters, flyers, and advertisements in traditional media. Institutions that seek to go beyond their customary audience must use newer technologies—educational and professional websites, portals, search engines, social media, and e-mail messages sent to acquired or shared databases. Of course, schools that aim to appeal to a regional audience must also engage in Internet marketing to achieve their ends, but prospective students for online programs are more likely to be found on the Internet. Schools that enter the online marketplace find that the largest fraction of students enrolling in their new online programs is drawn from nearby communities. While your administration may have projected substantially increased enrollments from remote students, colleges soon discover that virtual students are attracted to a school's digital programs largely for the same reason as their on-campus students—local reputation. Over time, and with wider and more sophisticated e-commerce recruitment techniques—if your online programs rise in stature in the US and abroad—greater numbers of distant students will enroll. Expect at first that most of your virtual student population will be regional—local students who are just as attracted to your programs as those who enroll on campus, but given various obstacles, are prevented from coming to campus.

While many US universities have increased on-campus enrollments by successfully recruiting international students—significantly from India and China and increasingly from Latin America, the Middle East, and Southeast Asia—the same experience does not hold online. Most students from abroad are attracted to US universities, not only for their reputation, but also—and perhaps most importantly—to absorb American culture and as a potential pathway to future employment in the US or in their home country. International students are not commonly drawn to online education, because for them, it does not appear to support close, long-term collegial connections and relationships they prize. In China, *guanxi* thrives on personal networks of influence, a central cultural idea originating with Confucianism, emphasizing mutual obligations, reciprocity, and trust—cultural norms that seem to international students to be antithetical to digital education.

The most successful schools offer nearly identical programs on-campus and online to students with academic profiles much the same as those who attend conventional classes. Students tend to select an institution—whether on-campus or online—not only because of its reputation, but crucially because programs match their educational or career objectives. A number of notable universities that entered online education early during the "dot-com" boom, created programs independent of their faculty, offering courses delivered by instructors from outside the institution. They introduced educational programs with which they had not been identified historically. By and large, they did not succeed. The most visible failures are several elite US universities that offered programs that diverged markedly from those for which the schools had been most noted. For most universities, it is strategically wiser to follow well-trodden academic paths, staying close to an institution's strengths, pursuing its historical mission while satisfying its natural audience, whether at a distance or at home.

Digital libraries, online registration, and other services have transformed the campus experience, not only for distance learners, but surprisingly for the residential population, too. Course management systems and other software now make it possible for students and faculty to communicate with one another, not only over long distances, but also to provide a convenient supplement to classroom instruction. Many schools that do not offer distance-learning programs nonetheless have introduced digital opportunities for on-campus faculty to post syllabi, course materials, and other documents. Exploiting learning management systems (LMS), conventional classroom teachers can communicate with their students after class in online discussion groups, require students to submit homework assignments online, and post grades and other data on class websites. Squeezed by shrinking budgets, schools can now offer virtual instruction, freeing classroom space by migrating one or more on-campus classes online in what is known as "hybrid" or "blended" programs, with some instruction performed in the classroom and the rest online. Recently, "flipped" classrooms, which provide residential students with lectures delivered online, reverse conventional classroom experience, with instruction presented virtually, while students—guided by faculty—explore concepts in class with their peers. Some hybrid classes, known as "low-residential" programs, offer online courses during most of the semester, with face-to-face lessons on weekends or summers. MOOCs—massive open online courses—deliver traditional lectures, video streamed worldwide to millions of students. Mostly free, but increasingly offered at a modest fee to earn certificates, they are commonly non-credit courses, taught largely by faculty at traditional universities. Most MOOCs deliver conventional course content, with some providing interactive student forums where students, professors, and teaching assistants communicate. At some colleges, MOOCs are suggested as supplemental content in conventional on-campus courses. Some schools offer self-learning online modules that demonstrate technical or other skills, which may not require classroom lectures or discussion, with courses similar to those available online at Khan Academy (www.khanacademy.org/), delivering practice exercises and instructional videos, giving students the chance to study at their own pace outside the classroom.

Online education is not one thing. As Table 7.2 shows, it comes in many flavors, depending on broader institution objectives, academic department aims, or for the purposes of other stakeholders. Entirely online programs that offer full degrees require substantial commitment from academic departments, faculty, technology services, and other personnel. At most institutions, digital degrees must be approved by a long chain of oversight bodies—department and school-wide faculty committees, and ultimately, in most US states, the state's department of education. In some fields, additional review is required from discipline-based accrediting bodies. If you are confronted with faculty and institutional resistance, it's a long slog to achieve approval for your first online degree. But once you make it through with your next and subsequent programs, the climb tends to be far less steep. One Master's degree at NYU Tandon School of Engineering was delayed interminably at the state because officials did not understand how it was possible for students to perform laboratory experiments online, convinced that the lab experience was possible on-campus only. In the end, the state approved

Table 7.2 Online Learning Modes

	Instruction	Location	On-campus attendance
Entirely online	Instructor-led	Virtual	None
Hybrid, blended, "flipped"	Instructor-led	Virtual and campus	Partly on-campus
Self-learning	No instructor*	Virtual	None
MOOCs	Instructor-led	Virtual	None

*Some self-learning "modules," often used in corporate training, provide mentors who communicate with students by e-mail or telephone.

the degree after we demonstrated how students performed hands-on operations as in a video game, simply by touching a computer screen or typing on a key pad. Physical presence was not required. In industry today, most operations are manipulated remotely and do not need direct physical contact. Automated industrial operations rarely depend on workers turning gears or pushing buttons on the factory floor.

To build a sustainable online program, you must fully engage the faculty. At the start, it's best to approach academic departments to gauge their interest, conferring with chairs to learn their reaction. Do they think faculty will support virtual instruction? Or do they think it will encounter serious resistance? Most of all, does the department head have sufficient confidence in digital learning to encourage faculty to embrace it? Since only a handful of departments will be willing to entertain your overture, let alone consider taking the next perilous step, it's wise to approach those who you suspect—based on their more adventurous practices in other spheres—will be likely to welcome you. While your strongest allies are enthusiastic department heads, some may give you merely lukewarm support. Failing to enlist a committed academic department chair, your next best ally is a noted scholar, someone who commands respect for solid research and institutional stature. Since they are not easy to attract, you will need to exercise your most persuasive arguments to gain their trust to champion your cause. Lacking a strong department head or notable scholar on your side, most faculty will be reluctant to step up, concluding that the department is not fully behind you. Faculty have other things to do with their very limited time—research being their principal commitment—with virtual instruction not only far less urgent, but may inhibit their academic success (see Chapter 5).

At a noted university, a number of years ago, I was invited to launch several new online degrees. I began by arranging appointments with academic department heads. At my first interview, I asked the chair whether he'd be interested in exploring online courses.

"No," he replied quietly but firmly, relaxing in his sun-filled office.

"Do you know what an online course is like?," I asked.

"No," he confirmed, easing more comfortably in his chair.

"Would you like me to give you access to one so that you can judge what it's like?," I asked.

"No," he concluded, ending our interview.

Taken aback, I recognized that this was not the department destined to lead the way. I forged on nonetheless, finding a wide range of interest elsewhere—from modest curiosity to eager participation. But even if you find willing partners, things will rarely proceed smoothly, largely because department heads already juggle other responsibilities that will distract them from taking on yet another burden. The role of a university department chair is not easy. Like the CEO of a small company, they must run complex enterprises, often with limited resources.

Apprehensive about enrollments and research funding, among other administrative frustrations, they are not often eager to assume yet another load.

In introducing your first new digital program, it's prudent to propose one that parallels an existing on-campus curriculum. Since your academic department, as well as university and accrediting bodies have blessed it on campus, chances are you will be asked to justify your new program's online delivery, but not its content. It's equally wise to introduce online versions of strong face-to-face courses with a history of attracting substantial enrollments. Since it has been market-tested, launching a new virtual program in the wake of robust enthusiasm for its face-to-face precursor, gives you a degree of confidence that your online alternative will succeed as well. Some schools have gone online, hoping to salvage weak programs. Audiences are unlikely to expand merely because you added another method of delivery. If a program is shaky face-to-face, offering it virtually will rarely increase broader acceptance. Once your virtual program is approved, however, you will gain confidence as you move others through review. You'll then be in a stronger position to propose less conventional disciplines, not commonly found on-campus. To guard against objections that your potential new, innovative degree falls outside standard academic practice, it's best to fold it under the umbrella of a classic academic department with a strong scholarly reputation. Under its authority, you will avoid suspicion that what you have in mind is too extreme. An unexpected benefit of new online initiatives is their departure from the commonplace. Freed from academic convention, you may find partners willing to join you to explore advances in emerging fields—collaborating with other academic departments online, for example, or even reaching out to other universities to initiate cross-disciplinary studies.

Unlike face-to-face teaching, a method that has followed a standard pattern across most institutions for centuries, there is no typical organization in virtual instruction. Because digital education emerged piecemeal over the last couple of decades, universities have adopted radically different structures. Like biological organisms, virtual governance has developed and grown in response to environmental factors—local academic norms, community needs, and institutional constraints. Some schools centralize online education under the provost's office; others are run by the school's information technology (IT) division. At still others, individual academic departments operate their own online units. Some universities support separate online entities at each school. At NYU, for example, medicine, law, and engineering each manage their own units, with additional support from IT and the provost. Pennsylvania State University introduced a standalone, nonprofit online school, Penn State World Campus, one of the strongest and most notable in the nation. Similarly, Drexel Online also manages a standalone digital school, but operates it as a for-profit company. At small liberal arts colleges, instructors are often free to offer online courses on their own, with little or no oversight. Many adventurous faculty adopt open-source technologies to move out on their own. At other schools, virtual instruction may be delivered as part of approved degrees only. Between the laissez-faire style of some schools and the more formal approach taken by others, digital instruction occurs in almost every corner of the modern university—as modules in face-to-face classes, as for-credit courses, in executive education, even in PhD programs. Historically, digital education evolved at many universities out of continuing education schools and remains so at many institutions today.

To go from state approval to online delivery, your institution must introduce a virtual education machine with many moving parts—faculty training, instructional technology support, student recruitment, and online student services, turning many digital educational gears to introduce a degree that is equal—if not superior—to what is available on campus. Figure 7.1 shows an example of staffing needs at NYU Tandon Online, the virtual education division of NYU's Engineering School. Since digital instruction units do not follow a common structure, the illustration is not presented as a model, but reflects various elements that many online learning units need to support digital instruction at their institutions. At Tandon Online, senior leadership is provided by the Online Faculty Oversight Committee, a group that meets twice a year to determine policy, review finances, set faculty compensation, and oversee quality. Chaired by the Dean, its members include academic chairs whose departments offer the school's online degrees, plus other senior faculty and staff, including the Vice Dean for Online Learning, whose staff provide various digital services to students and faculty.

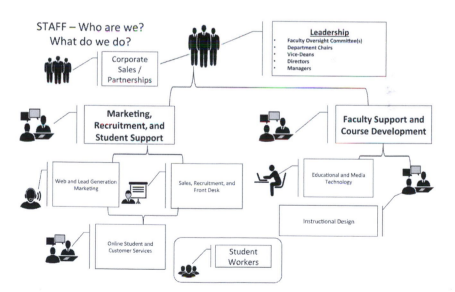

Figure 7.1 Online Learning Unit Staffing

Figure 7.1 is by John Vivolo, NYU Tandon School of Engineering.

The unit is divided into two principal operations—on the left, marketing, recruitment, and student support; on the right, faculty support and course development. A third function, corporate sales and partnerships, is shown in the upper-left-hand corner. Student workers, indicated at the bottom of the chart, are not only part of the team to support full-time staff, but offer faculty and staff insight into student preferences. Not indicated is a separate external advisory committee, the unit's Enterprise Learning Board (http://engineering.nyu.edu/enterprise-learning/board), with members reflecting various constituencies—digital learning experts, scholars, intellectual property attorneys, human resources officials, and corporate executives.

While students who walk into a conventional classroom at one school will find much the same configuration at any other anywhere in the nation or abroad—whether on an Ivy League campus or at local community college—online, the student experience is strikingly more fluid from one school to the next, from class to class. Paralleling wide differences in virtual governance, there are equally significant differences in scale and delivery in online courses. At Columbia University's Fu Foundation School of Engineering and Applied Science in Manhattan, for example, all online graduate courses are videostreamed. Just across the river in Brooklyn, at NYU Tandon School of Engineering, similar content is delivered in a style known as "active learning" (see Chapter 3). Elsewhere, digital courses are offered partly as instructional games, as videoconferencing, animation, simulations, or in any of dozens other technical and pedagogical approaches. While some play videos, others show slides with audio voiceover. In virtual instruction, there is no univeral mandate to follow a commonly accepted standard. Lacking a single method gives virtual education freedom to experiment with new learning modalities—adaptive, active, collaborative, and project-based learning, among others not commonly explored on campus.

Most universities tend to be ambivalent about digital education. University presidents are drawn largely from notable faculty, senior professors who earned their stature from scholarly achievement, who delivered lectures over their academic careers in trraditional classrooms and lecture halls. It's unlikely that more than a smattering of the nation's senior faculty have ever taught or taken classes online. Research reveals that the higher up the academic ladder, the less support virtual education receives from faculty. It's perfectly understandable that top adminsitrators at most schools are uneasy about online learning, either rejecting it altogether or proceeding very cautiously. Deciding whether to go online, university leadership faces conflicting pressures. At most instiutions, they will confront opposition (see Chapter 5) from conservative faculty, urging schools to tip-toe in at best, with many insisting that they stay out altogether. Political allies and trustees, often drawn from business circles, tend to encourage schools to move aggressively. To avoid conflict, some universities step in cautiously, taking a position somewhere between going fully online and doing nothing, a direction that appears to reconcile the irreconcilable. To be safe, a few schools have introduced "technology-mediated" instruction, offering "blended" learning elements to on-campus students. Exploiting this strategy, trustees may be mollified with the appearance that the school is actually delivering online instruction when only a few experience virtual instruction in selected classes in which a small number of adventurous teachers are prepared to experiment. With technology-mediated classes, the rest of the faculty is relieved, not having to participate when online instruction stops at the periphery, without invading the core, degree-granting curriculum. Technology-mediated courses, with merely a few instructors taking on the challenge, avoid the far-more complex and engaged practice of introducing fully online degrees to remote students. When faculty teach digital components in isolated, face-to-face classrooms, they withdraw from entering a broader, shared experience with other virtual intructors.

Most of us assume that universities are vastly different from corporations; that industry operates altogether differently under strict hierarchy, ruled largely in a top-down culture. In contrast, we imagine that faculty at colleges and universities are under no obligation to accept the mandates of those at the top. Academic freedom guarantees that faculty can follow their own paths, making their own way. Under closer examination, however, differences between corporate and academic life are not as great as we think. In industry, the chain of command is relatively straightforward, with the CEO at the top, the workforce falling largely into place. Conformity in the academy is far more subtlely achieved. Academic leaders rarely give direct orders. They make their wishes known circuitously, setting a tone, hinting about what they wish to accomplish. Faculty acceptance of indirect cues is observed when university administration change course. Schools that once encouraged virtual education under previous leadership can unexpectedly turn about-face, abandoning digital learning when a new president is appointed. At one notable school, once known as an innovator in digital education in a previous adminstration, soon retreated altogether when a new president was appointed. Under new leadership, it quickly pulled away, with most faculty quietly complying. In other examples, solid leadership can build nearly universal acceptance of virtual instruction. Arizona State University and Southern New Hampshire University are two examples of schools that have pulled ahead with strong online programs, accompanied by largely enthusiastic support from their academic communities. At most universities, conformity is never imposed; it's driven by inevitable acquiescence.

Cost-Effectiveness

By and large, colleges and universities charge the same tuition fee on-campus and online. The practice follows the principle that if the programs offer the same content, with the same or equally qualified faculty, eventually reporting the same outcomes, there should be no difference in tuition either. Some schools tack on a "technology fee" to recover some of the additional cost that the institution may have invested in digital education. But on the whole, schools have concluded that the perception of equivalence can be undermined if schools introduce a different tuition schedule for the two modes. Still, online education gives colleges the opportunity to experiment with alternative tuition models, with a handful offering partially or entirely online degrees at radically reduced or no tuition[8].

The few schools that reported financial failures after fairly large investments in online education often ignored sound business practices. In some cases, spending for course development and infrastructure was so great that it would have been impossible to earn back investments for years—if ever. Some spent as much as $250,000 on a single course. Others invested several million dollars in course management software. More prudent schools have wisely chosen to be cautious, investing modestly in course development and information technology. In the end, just like any responsible enterprise, sound financial planning and cautious investments in personnel and technology, coupled with modest revenue projections, protect fledgling online ventures from economic failure. Surprisingly, technology is not the principal ingredient in online learning. By now, a wide variety of quality courseware management systems are available from commercial vendors, often at licensing fees that are not impossible to manage. In selecting one, it is wise to engage faculty and technology staff in reaching a decision, keeping in mind the ease of use and compatibility with other campus systems, not only price. Most LMS's offer a suite of software options that provide nearly all tools that faculty and students need to communicate effectively—uploading, downloading, and sharing documents, slides, videos and other files; e-mailing individual students or the entire class collectively or an online team; managing threaded discussions; and accessing online bulletin boards. Other applications include student registration, scheduling, calendars, and the ability to mount quizzes and examinations. A key feature allows instructors to post grades for students to access online. Today, many schools have introduced systems that permit faculty and instructional designers to create, store, manage, and deliver digital content from a central repository (see Chapter 3). Most systems today integrate seamlessly with videoconferencing and other communication tools that offer real-time interaction. Vendors compete with one another to achieve an acceptable package, incorporating the latest and most user-friendly applications at a competitive price. If a school selects one of the principal brands, there is a good chance that the software, service, and price will be very close to the others. The cost of software that manages online learning represents a fraction of what institutions spend on information technology more generally. Licensing fees for course software usually occupy only a small portion of expenses—with faculty compensation being the biggest—that make up the bill for an online education program.

For smaller and mid-sized schools, it may be wise to consider sharing resources in consortia, such as Sakai (https://sakaiproject.org/), an open courseware organization with more than 350 member institutions worldwide. Or it may be prudent to allow a more experienced or larger university to handle software and infrastructure necessary to run a smooth operation. Some vendors will provide just your course management system, others hosting, and still others faculty training. Recently, a new category of commercial services has entered the market—vendors who provide universities with turn-key operations, including faculty training, course building, and marketing. Known as "enablers," or online program management (OPM) providers, they help colleges finance, mount and deliver programs online, taking a share of tuition revenue in return. Sums required to introduce course management systems, specialized software, and other information technology and training personnel add new lines to an institution's already thin budget. But when these allocations are measured against the vastly more expensive burden of building and maintaining campus dormitories, parking lots, athletic facilities, and other structures and services required to house a campus population, the cost of supporting online infrastructure and students is small. According to the OLC guidelines, cost-effectiveness must be attuned to institutional goals, while tuition and fees reflect the cost of delivering services.

Faculty Satisfaction

In part because of resistance by some faculty to online instruction—with many believing that online learning will corrupt the quality of higher education—most schools do not *require* that faculty teach online (see Chapter 5). Rather, they encourage them to teach virtual courses voluntarily. Early adopters often enter immediately, eager to master the challenges, to be at the leading edge of pedagogy. Frequently, they emerge as proselytizers, informing the rest of the community about their positive experiences. Curiously, many who teach online after strong resistance often join the ranks of the newly converted and are among the most vocal supporters. Many adapt what they discovered teaching online to their on-campus classes. In time, those who occupy the middle ground with a "wait-and-see" attitude may drift into the online learning camp as some of us do eventually when new technologies are at first dismissed and then widely adopted.

Online faculty compensation often parallels what professors are paid on campus. Some institutions provide economic and other incentives to teach online. At NYU Tandon School of Engineering, online instructors are compensated separately for developing a digital course and for teaching it. A number of schools present digital faculty with laptops or give them release time from their normal teaching load to encourage them to migrate their face-to-face courses to virtual instruction. Once a faculty member agrees to teach online, in most cases, the university steps in to offer online teaching instruction. At some schools, faculty training falls under the arm of IT. At others, it is handled by a separate online learning unit. No matter where responsibility rests, online faculty training is a major departure from traditional university teaching. Historically, most college faculty enter the physical classroom with little or no pedagogical knowledge. When online education was first introduced, faculty were encouraged, not only to absorb new online teaching practices—peer-to-peer, group, project-based, and other innovative learning techniques—but also to master digital technologies—multimedia software, video streaming, and webinar tools, among other applications. Today, however, recognizing that faculty are experts at content, but may not be skilled at manipulating online software, colleges have introduced a new breed of specialists who assume responsibility for translating faculty knowledge into sophisticated, interactive presentations. Known as instructional technologists, they use authoring tools to illuminate concepts with text, audio, images, animation, video, and interactive content (see Chapter 5).

Among the thorniest issues facing academic institutions since the introduction of online learning is that of intellectual property. Who owns the rights to Web-based courses? Should copyright be in the name of the developer or the university? If a school engages faculty to develop online courses, may the institution have someone else teach them? Do digital faculty have portability rights, allowing them to take their e-courses when they leave? Should schools pay course developers separately from their normal compensation as faculty? Should faculty be compensated separately for online instruction? Although these questions seemed intractable at first, many universities have come to an accommodation with their faculty. A few institutions have concluded that the university owns all the rights, including copyright. Others give copyright to the faculty. Most have decided to share ownership. One solution (see Chapter 8), widely adopted by colleges and universities, provides for the faculty to retain all rights in the course, apart from online instruction, allowing them freedom to teach face-to-face, publish, consult, or perform any other academic task with the material. In return, course developers voluntarily transfer their rights to the online course to the university. In this way, the faculty retains its traditional academic freedom, while schools gain the right to commercialize Web-based courses.

Student Satisfaction

At the conclusion of most college and university courses, students are asked to complete paper-based surveys evaluating their classroom experience, reporting on their perceptions of how well faculty performed as well as whether students accomplished what they set out to achieve, among other perceptions of the value of each course. In order to gauge the effectiveness of online education, students at a distance must perform similar evaluations. In the largest continuing study of student perceptions of their online courses, performed at the SUNY Learning Network, most students reported that their online experience was equal to, or better than, that in traditional classrooms[9].

To achieve such results, the most successful schools have introduced online student services that provide nearly all the elements that the campus population has come to expect. At NYU Tandon School of Engineering, for example, virtual students can accomplish nearly everything online that their peers do routinely on campus—apply and register, get academic advice, buy textbooks, pay tuition, gain access to the school's digital library, and perform course evaluations. An Eduventures report[10] concludes that virtual education must offer a wide range of features to remote students in order to fulfill their expectations—engaging and interactive presentations, communication forums, around-the-clock student support, seamless transactions. According to OLC, "Students are successful in learning online and typically pleased with their experience." On the whole, the literature supports that claim[11]. Students appear satisfied when there is robust online discussion with their instructors and classmates, when their online learning experience matches their expectations; when university services—advising, registration, and access to materials—is at least as good as those provided on campus. Institutions that offer online students effective digital orientation sessions about how to learn online and whose educational outcomes provide seamless pathways to successful careers and educational attainment emerge as leaders in online education.

Success in online learning depends crucially on thoughtful planning and sound research. Above all, it requires broad academic and administrative participation. Before the first course is delivered online, institutions must come to terms with how it might affect all walks of university life—students, faculty, finance, admissions, IT, the library, trustees, even the bookstore. Of course, being too cautious can lead to academic paralysis. Schools that select a champion who commands respect among faculty and staff can help navigate competing interests to achieve consensus and help move things forward[12]. Perhaps the most significant predictor of success is institutional commitment—financial, technical, and legal— in an atmosphere, articulated at the highest levels, that supports and encourages online education.

Notes

1 See Online Learning Consortium Member Catalog of Online Programs at http://olc. onlinelearningconsortium.org/onlineprogram_listing.

2 Headings in this essay are drawn from OLC's Five Pillars of Quality Online Education at http://onlinelearningconsortium.org/about/quality-framework-five-pillars/. See also *Elements of Quality: The Sloan-C Framework*. (2002). New York: Alfred P. Sloan Foundation.

3 Russell, T. L. (2001). *The no significant difference phenomenon* (5th ed.). IDECC. Retrieved from http://nosignificantdifference.org/.

4 See, for example, *Characteristics of Excellence in Higher Education: Eligibility Requirements and Standards for Accreditation*. (2002). Philadelphia: Middle States Commission on Higher Education.

5 Means, B., Toyama, Y., Murphy, R., Bakia, M. & Jones, K. (2009). *Evaluation of evidence-based practices in online learning: A meta-analysis and review of online learning studies*. U.S. Department of Education.

6 National Center for Educational Statistics. (2002 October). *Projections for educational statistics to 2012* (31st ed.). Washington, DC: U.S. Department of Education.

7 Gallagher, Sean. (2002 September). Distance learning at the tipping point. *Eduventures Report.*
8 Kelley, K. B. & Bonner, K. M. (2001 February). Courseware ownership in distance learning: issues and policies. *Sloan Consortium Newsletter.*
9 Fredericksen, E., Pickett, A., Shea, P. & Pelz, W. (2000). Student satisfaction and perceived learning with online courses: Principles and examples from the SUNY learning network. *JALN, 4*(2).
10 Gallagher, S. (2002 September). Distance learning at the tipping point. *Eduventures Report.*
11 Effective Practices Sorted by Pillar—Student Satisfaction at http://olc.onlinelearning consortium.org/ep_by_pillar_ss?page=3.
12 Hezel, R. T. (2002 October). How to plan for your institution's distance learning efforts. *Educational Pathways.*

This is an edited version of an entry, co-authored with Frank Mayadas, published in The Encyclopedia of Distributed Learning, *SAGE Publications (2004) as "Online Learning Environments," pp. 345–356.*

8

WHO OWNS WHAT?

Unbundling Online Course Property Rights

A tug-of-war between faculty and administration over who owns online courses has been taking place on our nation's campuses. Pulling forcefully on one end are those institutions that declare that because they paid faculty to develop online courses and because they invested in educational technology software, supported instructional training and design, and absorbed most other costs, online courses belong to the university. Tugging at the other end are faculty who say that because they created digital courses, copyright law, and academic convention support their right to ownership, no different from on-campus courses. Virtual classes, they argue, belong entirely to the faculty.

In a survey I conducted,[1] about half the schools that offer online courses reported that their institutions have a digital course intellectual property policy in place. At a quarter of these, the schools own all online course rights. Just over 10 percent said that their faculty own the rights, while another third reported that faculty and the university share them. Half the schools said they haven't yet instituted a policy or are in the midst of devising one. As expected, the results show little or no consensus. While the growth of online education learning has taken off, many institutions haven't yet decided when to offer online courses, let alone whether to enter a political struggle with faculty over rights. Schools considering introducing virtual classes face other hurdles first—selecting the right online learning software, training digital instructors, choosing which courses to offer, and calculating how to compensate faculty for developing virtual courses and teaching online, among dozens of other difficult tasks. Recognizing that Stevens Institute of Technology's long-established intellectual property policies failed to account for online courses, the school appointed a faculty committee to explore online course ownership and to recommend a new policy. Composed of veteran and junior members, the group first met in the summer of 1999.[2]

As the director of WebCampus.Stevens, the graduate school's online learning program, I was named as the chair.

Ownership, Use, and Compensation

In preparing for our work, the committee searched the relatively sparse online learning rights literature, collected a few useful virtual course ownership policies in place at other colleges, and generated a list of key issues we felt needed study. We divided these into ownership, use, and compensation.

"Who owns the rights to online courses?" covers these thorny issues:

- When institutions market and distribute virtual courses, who owns the rights?
- Should copyright be in the name of the digital course developer or the university?
- Under which conditions, if any, may copyright be assigned to the school?

Turning to use,

- If a school engages faculty to develop online courses, may the institution engage someone else to teach them?
- May the university license online courses to third parties, such as other schools, publishers, or distributors?
- Do digital faculty have portability rights, allowing them to take their virtual courses when they leave?

As for compensation, should schools pay online course developers separately from their normal compensation as faculty? Should faculty be compensated separately for online instruction?

If course developers receive portability rights—that is, if they can teach their virtual courses elsewhere—should the next school or commercial enterprise compensate the originating college?

- Should developers receive additional payment in the event the school licenses online courses?
- In the event that another faculty member at the originating school teaches an existing online course, should the original developer receive extra compensation?

Digging into the literature, we found, as expected, that some had already rushed in, either to protect their vulnerable interests or to explore the new territory.

Among others, copyright experts, faculty unions, college administrators, and elected officials had weighed in with their observations, many sensibly, a few recklessly.

Unbundling

Luckily, our group found some serious work already done. The most impressive was a study of "unbundling," a concept first articulated for digital courses by CETUS, the widely influential consortium jointly sponsored by California State University, State University of New York, and City University of New York[3]. Among other things, unbundling acknowledges that rights are both extendable and divisible, and that they exist in the context of relationships. Unbundling recognizes that an instructional object—lecture notes, for example, or quizzes and the like—can have many attributes and uses. Consider a slide presentation. Illustrations can be displayed on a screen for classroom instruction, submitted for publication in a periodical, or published in a textbook. They may also accompany a talk at a technical conference. In an online course, students all over the world can click on them. An instructional object can assume various identities, like an actor playing different roles, depending on where it's used. Unbundling proposes that different parties can own such versatile learning objects when they perform different functions on separate academic or scholarly stages—in the classroom or online. Not only can they be used differently, but copyright law gives the owner the right to sell objects separately.

Publishing

Traditional scholarly publishing also offered policies adaptable to virtual education. For centuries, academics have voluntarily given certain rights to commercial or university presses because they appreciate that publishers possess the market power to stock bookstore and library shelves. In exchange, authors benefit by earning royalties or by having their intellectual effort disseminated globally in the scholarly literature. Publishing also acknowledges the divisibility of rights. Contracts usually call for authors to assign limited rights to publishers. In certain agreements, authors assign their rights for North American publication only, retaining foreign rights for themselves. Or, they give the publisher the right to the hard-cover edition only, with paperback rights reserved for the author. Freelance writers commonly give publishers rights for their stories to appear in a magazine once only. The writer retains any remaining rights—reprinting, adaptation, and translation, among others.

Distinctions

Our committee articulated a number of distinctions we thought important. At the faculty end of online learning is intellectual content, created by course developers. These syllabi, lecture notes, bibliographies, reading selections, videos, examinations, and other elements constitute a string of instructional objects that can be used on-campus, online, and in other ways. At the institutional end is commercialization, with activities such as marketing, distribution, licensing, and management, among other services. These also include technical and e-commerce infrastructure provided by the school. We also believed it important to distinguish between supplementary course modules, created by faculty to support conventional classroom teaching as well as entirely online courses, delivered to students exclusively over the Internet, with no (or limited) face-to-face instruction. Finally, we recognized that virtual faculty engage in two distinct functions. They develop instructional objects for delivery over the Internet and they teach online.

In the end, our committee proposed the following key recommendations. By unbundling different rights and uses, the policy recognizes the sometimes competing claims of faculty and academic institutions to intellectual property contained in virtual courses.

Online Course Ownership Policy Recommendations

Copyright. A course developer's copyright to an entirely online course should be assigned to the school when the faculty member agrees to enter a contract with the institution to develop it.

Compensation. The agreement should compensate developers for creating entirely online courses in "virtual space"—a provision that should not apply to online material presented in conventional classrooms in "physical space." Faculty should also be compensated separately for entirely online instruction.

Use. While copyright for an entirely online course is assigned to the university, the faculty member retains the unlimited right to use course material components (notes, slides, videos, databases, exercises, and so on) for other purposes, such as conventional classroom teaching, publication, lectures, consulting, among other activities.

Portability. In the event the developer delivers an entirely online course at other schools, a usage license fee should be paid to the originating institution.

Third-party Licensing. If an entirely online course is licensed to a third party—publisher, corporation, distributor, or other school—the course developer should receive a percentage of the net licensing revenue.

Additional Compensation. If an entirely online course is taught at the originating school by someone other than the developer, the faculty member who created it should receive a percentage of the net tuition revenue.

In November 2000, after our recommendations had gone through a year of review by faculty, staff, and trustee panels, Stevens' faculty endorsed what our group believed was one of the most liberal online course policies introduced in the nation's colleges. In February 2001, Stevens' Board of Trustees adopted it as the school's official online learning intellectual property rights policy. It took more than 18 months for it to navigate through Stevens' academic channels—and we believe it was worth the wait. The new rules were announced in November 2000 at a conference at the University of Maryland[4]. Experts who attended the Sloan Foundation-sponsored meeting applauded Stevens' solution. One senior college administrator claimed that the school's model "appears to have solved the question of Web course ownership in our universities."

The policy is both academically fair and economically just. Faculty receive reasonable compensation for their intellectual contributions, not only from online development and instruction, but also from projected income streams that may flow from licensing and other revenue sources. The policy also gives faculty complete academic freedom over learning objects they create for scholarship and teaching outside of digital courses. What's more, universities—which may have invested heavily in virtual education and its marketing and licensing—can enter the digital learning marketplace confidently, their rights and potential income protected as well.

Notes

1   The results are from an online survey of Web-based distance learning programs at US colleges and universities conducted from November 20, 2000 to December 13, 2000.
2   Members of Stevens' Ad Hoc Committee on Web-based Intellectual Property Rights are Stanley Clark, Dilhan Kalyon, Lawrence Levine, David Naumann, Keith Sheppard, and Robert Ubell (chair). The committee was formed by the Graduate School Vice President Joseph J. Moeller, Jr. and School of Engineering Dean Bernard Gallois.
3   Consortium for Educational Technology for University Systems, *Ownership of New Works at the University: Unbundling of Rights and the Pursuit of Higher Learning* (California State University, 1997).
4   R. Ubell, "Unbundling Intellectual Property: Recognizing Rights in Distance Learning," delivered at the 6th International Conference on Asynchronous Learning Networks, held on November 3–5, 2000 at the University of Maryland in College Park, Md.

This essay is a slightly edited version of an article that appeared first in Educause Quarterly, *No. 1, 2001, pp. 45–47.*

9

THE ROAD NOT TAKEN

Divergence of Corporate and Academic Online Instruction

In a Robert Frost poem, a traveler suddenly comes upon two roads diverging in a forest. Setting out one way, he regrets that he "could not travel both." With a sigh, he doubts he will ever return to explore the road not taken[1]. If you take one path, you never know what might have happened if you went another way. Curiously, two recent pathways—corporate and academic digital learning—each taking a separate road, give us an opportunity to retrace steps.

In the lab, scientists can manipulate variables, open lines of comparison, or establish controls. But in life, such experiments are quite rare. As it happens, computer-mediated learning is an unusual instance that allows us to compare parallel tracks *in vivo*. Both corporate and university online learning were launched at about the same time and continued separately, more or less independently for more than a decade. Both have turned out to be surprisingly successful. Uncannily, both corporate e-learning and academic online learning[2] have penetrated about a quarter of their markets[3,4]. Why did they diverge? What accounts for corporate e-learning going off in one direction, while higher education went in another?

What's the Difference?

Looking back, we can trace two clearly distinct histories and philosophies. Companies chose e-learning, a portfolio of virtual, self-learning modules for workers to complete on their own; universities adopted an altogether different style, largely mirroring the classroom in an instructor-led collaborative environment. At first glance, academic online and corporate e-learning appear the same. Workers at companies and students at universities all face computer screens or hold hand-held devices. Even at the back end, they are pretty much alike. Courses are mounted on learning management systems (LMS) that facilitate registration, usage, and completion data, and in universities, discussion boards, grade books, collaborative software, among other tools.

Few are aware that online learning at companies and in schools is quite distinct. Once instruction begins, they clearly fall into separate camps. At companies, e-learning is highly mediated by technology, with trainers disappearing entirely, replaced largely on monitors by instructional design elements, presented in text, multimedia, games, simulations, and other displays. In contrast, in online courses at universities—often equally media-rich—instructors and students take their virtual seats online, interacting continuously with one another in text and real time. Online, workers are on their own, while college students and faculty learn together[5]. When corporate learners face computer screens, they act autonomously, responding to commands or queries by themselves. But in an online college class, students and faculty interact, engaging in asynchronous or live conversations, often in teams (see Chapter 1).

Collaborative learning encourages knowledge creation through interaction, with participants actively sharing discoveries and experience. Based principally on theories proposed by early Soviet psychologist Lev Vygotsky, who believed that learning emerges naturally from social interaction[6], learners engage in common, mutually dependent tasks, leading to the creation of new or expanded knowledge. In higher education, teaming and peer-to-peer learning are now essential online practices. At universities, online collaboration reassembles traditional classroom relationships, placing students at the center of the stage, with instructors as observers and commentators in the wings (see Chapter 2). Although certain instructor-led virtual courses are offered in corporate settings, the lack of peer-to-peer instruction is especially surprising because teamwork is now so highly valued by industry as a productive force. Faced with flatter management structures and a globally distributed workforce, employees now routinely communicate with one another virtually. These trends have so far not yet been widely translated into learning options in corporations.

Along the Corporate Road to E-Learning

Digital learning in industry grows out of a long tradition of worker training, stretching back at least to the Second World War when it first became common practice. Moving from wartime factories to a peace economy, and especially following a period of rapid postwar technological advance, training became a requirement in virtually all industries. The introduction of computers further accelerated the demand. In corporations, e-learning reaches back to programmed instruction, introduced in the last century to build a skilled workforce. While Ohio State University psychologist Sidney L. Pressey may have been the first to engineer a device to drill students by exploiting immediate feedback[7], it was not until Harvard behaviorist B. F. Skinner championed his "teaching machine" that programmed instruction really took off. Based largely on concepts in behavioral psychology, programmed instruction provides self-paced learning, reinforced along a carefully managed sequence of tasks, leading to a set of predetermined goals. Skinner believed that learning constituted a cascade of stimulus-response events solidified by reinforcement. To achieve success and reduce error, he proposed that the learning process is best divided into "a very large number of very small steps and reinforcement must be contingent upon the accomplishment of each step.[8]"

When computers invaded industry, training officers immediately grasped their possibilities as powerful instruments for learning. Modeled on programmed instruction, computer-based training (CBT), provided linear, self-paced instruction, used mostly to teach standard processes, such as software programs[9]. Perfect for drill, practicing skills, and testing performance, CBT gave workers immediate feedback at the very moment when they acquire proficiency. Because they see results instantly, learners know right away whether they have absorbed the lesson. Crucially, CBT allow employees to return to problems they failed to master earlier, reworking them to increase their performance, and following Skinner, reinforcing their knowledge. E-learning is much livelier than its rather plain CBT cousin. Exploiting some of the same instructional concepts, the old CBTs take on a new life on the Internet—enhanced by simulations, video, games, and other multimedia applications. In this century, they morphed into e-learning modules. E-learning crested on the great Internet wave that swept over industry, transforming everything in its wake—manufacturing, product development, supply chain, marketing, customer service, and not least, the way training is delivered to a global workforce. With every phase of commerce captured online, inevitably, corporate learning was snagged too. Responsible for the most profound shift in work since the industrial revolution, the Internet—at first accelerated by the "dot-com" boom—also fueled corporate learning. In little over a decade, corporations moved rapidly from face-to-face instruction—as practically the only actor on the training stage—to sharing curriculum significantly with e-learning. The change was largely due to the overwhelming economic advantage of online instruction over conventional classroom teaching. Fierce economic forces have caused lavish country-club training parks to shut down, employee travel to exotic sites to be canceled, and tellingly for the bottom line, workers are now often kept at their desks or on the factory floor, participating in e-learning, rather than in classrooms, to increase productivity. E-learning has obviously been instrumental in supporting these trends. Web instruction has also helped propel worldwide corporate expansion. Self-learning modules are easily circulated to a globally scattered workforce at relatively low cost. As e-learning historian Paul Nicholson remarks, "E-learning in business and training [is] driven by notions of improved productivity and cost reduction, especially in an increasingly globalised business environment. . . .[10]"

The Parallel Road to Academic Online Learning

University online education is descended chiefly from distance education, a line that goes back to the mid-nineteenth century when Isaac Pitman first taught shorthand in England through the mail. In the US, correspondence schools flourished at the turn of the last century, especially after the University of Chicago launched "learning by correspondence" programs to thousands of students in the US and abroad[11]. Later, radio and television extended distance learning even further with the Open University in the UK being one of the first to exploit mass communication.

With computing, academic distance education finally came into its own. In the early 1960s, PLATO (Programmed Logic for Automatic Teaching Operations), built at the University of Illinois at Champaign-Urbana, was remarkably ahead for its day both pedagogically and technically. It was the first generalized computer-assisted instruction system[12]. Some of today's key academic online learning features had their early start with PLATO—forums, message boards, online testing, e-mail, chat, instant messaging, and multi-player games. Today, these early innovations are standard applications in university online education[13]. PLATO was succeeded by a string of software and communication advances, now housed on a handful of dominant LMSes. The ubiquity of the Internet not only made it possible for higher education to reach out to remote students and adult learners whose work and family lives prevented them from attending class on campus, but decisively allowed the key features drawn from traditional classroom instruction to flourish too. Virtual education made the vintage, one-on-one, faculty-student correspondence school model look quaint. It opened a space for one-to-many interactions and peer-to-peer learning, an unprecedented advance few had predicted[14]. Encouraged by the Alfred P. Sloan Foundation's program in Asynchronous Learning Networks (ALN) and by other philanthropies and government funding, online learning today has broadly entered mainstream higher education and is penetrating elementary and high schools as well.

A new Online Learning Consortium survey says that more than 5.8 million, or more than a quarter of the US higher education student population, were enrolled in at least one online course in the fall of 2014 [3].

The Internet immediately revealed its obvious economic advantages for training, but its implications for higher education were not as apparent at the start. Recently, however, it has not gone unnoticed by chief financial officers at academic institutions. Faced with continually diminished resources, colleges and universities have come to recognize the economic benefits institutions can achieve with virtual education. Online, students do not rely on hugely expensive campus infrastructure. Studying at home or on the job, they don't swim in campus pools or park their cars in vast lots. Neither do they live in boutique-style dorms or attend classes in smartly up-to-date academic buildings that require deep pockets to build and maintain. What's more, in blended learning, when students shuffle their schedules to attend some classes on campus and others online, colleges benefit by doubling-up on the use of limited classroom space, freeing budgets for other pressing academic needs. While corporate and academic learning continue to run largely on separate tracks, the clear cost benefits of online instruction are now recognized by both.

Separate Theoretical Paths

In advanced economies, corporate training emerges from a number of intertwined theories and traditions (see Table 9.1). Focusing on procedural, rather than conceptual knowledge, companies inevitably embraced behavioral approaches as an engine to build a skilled workforce.

Procedural knowledge means knowing how to manipulate a condition or how to perform a task; for example, how to run a science experiment or solve a mathematical equation. Procedural knowledge is also a measure of our skills, tasks we know how to complete, and techniques we know how to follow. Training is designed to give workers procedural knowledge in order for them to do their jobs effectively. Conceptual knowledge, on the other hand, refers to our ability to appreciate major parts in a system, understand complex relationships, or categorize elements logically. At their best, universities are expected to equip students to excel at conceptual knowledge.

Two major, opposing schools of thought have fought for ascendancy over the last century and are still in conflict today. Behaviorism[15], championed by B. F. Skinner and others, was largely adopted by corporations, while constructivism, initially led by John Dewey and other progressive educators, has emerged as the chief learning theory among online learning educators[16], even though it has not been widely adopted in traditional classrooms. Behaviorism claims that only objectively observable features of learning count, while constructivism sees learning as a process in which the learner actively builds knowledge (see Chapter 1). Yet the behaviorist impulse is not confined to corporate training alone. It pervades nearly every school from suburban kindergarten to elite universities, with testing, objective scores, and outcomes-based instruction at every level. Today, no classroom is immune from being measured for achievement, performance, rank, completion, and so on. While elementary and high schools

Table 9.1 Corporate and Academic Learning

Corporate E-Learning	Academic Online Learning
Training	Education
Procedural Learning	Conceptual Learning
Behaviorism	Constructivism
Autonomous	Collaborative

have been subject to a battery of assessments for years, higher education accreditors, who until recently have left colleges pretty much on their own to achieve their own aims, now demand that universities also produce measureable, evidence-based results. Even in academic online learning, the fairly secure home of constructivist practice, testing, and measurement burrow deeply into virtual classrooms.

The wall separating corporate and academic instruction is a pretty high jump, even though there are now some minor cracks. Social networking, Internet communities, blogs, podcasts, and other so-called Web 2.0 technologies shape the work experiences of employees everywhere. But even as many millions have joined Facebook, LinkedIn, and other social networks and participate in online communities, so far they fall outside the learning function at most companies. There is one place, however, where corporate and academic Web learning meet— at the crossroads of tuition reimbursement that US companies spend supporting personnel who enroll in accredited degree-granting programs as part of employee benefits packages. When colleges first offered online degrees, many companies frowned upon them, refusing to contribute to online tuition, claiming that the degrees were inferior. But recently, learning officers have come around to the other side, encouraging workers to enroll, recognizing the educational and personal benefits that make online education appealing. Some companies that are eager to build a cadre of talented specialists in fields that match their corporate objectives have targeted mission-critical online degrees for key employees. Even though there are modest indications that the wall between industry and academic learning is not as high as it once was, it's questionable whether the two roads will ever join. E-learning is a vehicle for training; online learning a platform for education. The two have quite different aims, and consequently, as we have seen, very different methods and philosophies. But as global demands require more agile workers who can go beyond being merely skilled at procedures and who can adapt flexibly to post-industrial markets[17], corporate training officers may yet turn to collaborative, peer-to-peer learning as a prudent option. Doubtless, right now, progressive corporate thinkers are exploring ways to absorb some of the positive lessons drawn from academic online learning in corporate e-learning instruction.

Notes

1 Throughout this essay, "e-learning" refers to *corporate* digital training, while "online learning" is the term used for *academic* virtual education.
2 Frost, R. (1969). The road not taken. In *The poetry of Robert Frost* (p. 105). New York, NY: Holt, Rinehart, and Winston.
3 ASTD. (2015). *2015 State of the industry report*. Alexandria, VA: ASTD.
4 Allen, I. E. & Seaman, J. (2016). *Online report card—tracking online education in the United States*, Online Learning Consortium. Retrieved from: http://onlinelearningsurvey.com/reports/changingcourse.pdf.

5 Hiltz, S. R. & Goldman, R. (2005). *Learning online together.* Mahwah, NJ: Lawrence Erlbaum.

6 Vygotsky, L. (1929). *The problem of the cultural development of the child.* Retrieved from: www.marxists.org/archive/vygotsky/index.htm.

7 Pressey, S. L. (1950). Development and appraisal of devices providing immediate automatic scoring of objective tests and concomitant self-instruction. *Journal of Psychology: Interdisciplinary and Applied, 29*(2), 417–447.

8 Skinner, B. F. (1954). The science of learning and the art of teaching. *Harvard Educational Review, 24,* 86–97.

9 Dean, C. & Whitlock, Q. (1983). *Handbook of computer-based training.* London: Kogan Page.

10 Nicholson, P. (2007). A history of E-learning. In B. Fernández-Manjón et al. (Ed.), *Computers and education: E-learning from theory to practice* (pp. 1–11). New York, NY: Springer Publishing Company.

11 Watkins, B. L. (1991). *The foundations of American distance learning.* Dubuque, IA: Kendall/Hunt.

12 Woolley, D. R. (1994). PLATO: The emergence of online community. *Matrix News,* January.

13 Sivunen, A., & Valo, M. (2010). Communication technologies. In Robert Ubell (Ed.), *Virtual teamwork.* Hoboken, NJ: John Wiley & Sons.

14 Some pre-Internet era visionaries who imagined virtual collaborative learning include futurist Buckminster Fuller, Stanford philosopher Kenneth Suppes, and American inventor Raymond Kurzweil.

15 Baum, W. (1994). *Understanding behaviorism.* New York: HarperCollins.

16 Dewey, J. (1915). *The school and society.* Chicago, IL: Chicago University Press.

17 Ambrose, J. Personal communication.

This essay first appeared as "The Road Not Taken: The Divergence of Corporate and Academic Web Instruction" in the Journal of Asynchronous Learning Networks, *November 2010, Vol. 14, No. 2, pp. 3–8.*

10

ENGINEERS TURN TO ONLINE LEARNING

"It's like teaching through a straw," winced an engineering professor who had just spent 13 weeks interacting on the Internet with a dozen graduate students. The members of his class, like millions of others worldwide who now take courses entirely online, downloaded his lecture notes, communicated with each other and their instructor through e-mail, and took exams by responding to questions on computer screens at home or at work. Even in the absence of face-to-face interactions in the classroom, these students found that the convenience of virtual education made learning through a straw very sweet.

Since before the days of Socrates, teaching has largely involved flesh-and-blood instructors lecturing to their students—beneath a tree, in a colonnaded stoa, or in a brick-and-mortar schoolroom. Today, thanks to widespread access to the Internet, online education is enabling professionals to learn from afar, keeping pace with technological and managerial changes, despite their heavy schedules. Online learning, especially for engineers and executives in technology industries, has emerged as one of the fastest-moving trends in higher education. Thousands of technical and management courses, including degree and certificate programs, are now being offered by universities, for-profit professional development centers, and industry training facilities worldwide.

To be sure, the ability to instruct from afar is hardly new. As early as the mid-1800s, correspondence schools in Europe were teaching shorthand and foreign languages by mail. In the last century, radio, television, and satellite broadcasting equipped distance learning with new methods of delivery (see Chapter 3). The global connectivity of the Internet and a new generation of hardware and software applications underpin the teaching of courses on the Internet. By almost any measure, digital education is booming. What many educators are realizing is that online learning is a trend they can no longer ignore.

The Engineer as an Online Learner

As any working engineer knows, there is tremendous pressure to keep pace with the latest technology and the newest ways of doing business. "Engineers tell me that they need a thorough refresher course in their specialties at least every other year," remarked Peter F. Drucker, the best-selling author and management guru. "And a 're-immersion'—their word—in the basics at least every four years." Yet few engineers have the luxury of attending classes on well-groomed college campuses. Even those who do enroll in graduate school often attend part-time in the evenings, rushing off to class after work, grabbing a bite along the way. When the bell rings at the end of class, they are soon back in the parking lot, speeding off for home. For these part-time learners—the lion's share of today's graduate population—the actual classroom can be far more alienating than the virtual one (see Chapter 5). "Traffic and parking are two of my biggest hassles," said Dean C. Reonieri Jr., a software developer at Lucent Technologies Inc. who has been taking online graduate courses from Stevens Institute of Technology in Hoboken, N.J. "The best thing about taking an online course for me is convenience," Gautham Natarajan at AT&T in New Jersey, agrees. He enrolled in two online telecommunications courses offered by Stevens last spring and found it "very flexible. I could access the courses whenever I wanted—at home, at work, wherever there was a computer nearby." Natarajan estimates that he saved 45 minutes in commuting each way.

The business world is also finding online learning to be a boon for employee training, especially as more corporations become global enterprises. One corporate training executive recalled that, not long ago, his mission was to provide classes for engineers in two or three sites in New Jersey. These days, he is responsible for training employees in several countries in Europe, Asia, Australia, and America. Some firms operate "corporate universities" online. Many of them collaborate with academic institutions to deliver courses straight out of the school catalog or produce customized courses. For-profit websites also fill the technical training niche, offering product-specific courses in computer applications. Lynda.com (https://lynda.com/) and Khan Academy (https://khanacademy.org/) are two of the most popular. MIT, Berkeley, Michigan, and other schools also offer free online technical courses. Free Massive Open Online Courses (MOOCs) from Coursera (https://coursera.org/) and EdX (https://edx.org/), delivered by dozens of accredited universities, are also available free or at a modest fee to earn a certificate.

Virtual Classroom

Just as in conventional classrooms, the day-to-day activities of online education vary widely. College and university virtual courses tend to follow the standard academic calendar, delivered over 12 to 15 weeks. At the start of the term, the instructor indicates what is required—whether and when students will take mid-term or final exams and submit problem sets or final projects—and how the course will be conducted. Commonly, the school will provide online orientation sessions, taking students through a typical online course, giving them hints on how to navigate their new virtual environment successfully, and—perhaps most importantly—how to manage study time prudently. Each course has its own homepage on the Web where the instructor posts class materials, such as lecture notes, homework problems, reading assignments, and video clips of lectures or demonstrations. Pedagogically, the Internet's archival ability is one of its great advantages over the classroom. In particular, it enables asynchronous learning—students can access the course website whenever and wherever convenient—at home before work, during lunch breaks at the office, or in the middle of the night. In some cases, though, students may need to log in at designated times for live webcasts of lectures or for chat sessions with classmates and instructors. Some courses also stipulate that students show up on campus for an initial meeting with the instructor and other students. For many digital learning courses, the class never meets in person. Instead, they communicate online—not just to hand in homework, but also to ask questions, comment on class topics, and respond to comments and questions from others. The instructor may even break-up the class into groups to work on team projects or reports, fostering what educators call collaborative learning, an interactive style of problem-solving that in many cases improves student understanding (see Chapter 1). "Without some kind of discussion, distance learning is pretty worthless," observed Howard R. Budin, former head of the Center for Technology and School Change at Columbia University's Teachers College. Like many virtual teachers, Budin weighs student grades by their degree of participation in online discussions. For the most part, however, online grades are still determined largely by how students do on exams and homework. At many schools, exams are conducted by vendors, such as ProctorU (http://proctoru.com/), who monitor students, observing them from remote sites on webcams installed in most laptops. Students interact with live proctors, who have access to student computer screens. To authenticate student identity, test-takers are asked to show a photo ID and answer a few questions generated from a public information database. At NYU Tandon School of Engineering, following thousands of successfully completed remotely proctored exams, less than a handful of students exhibited questionable behavior, and most cases were quickly resolved.

Sophisticated software is now available for designing, teaching, and administering a virtual course. Basic features include a user interface for uploading and downloading course material; sending and receiving e-mail; and grading exams, among other features. Most platforms also accommodate threaded discussions, chat rooms, bulletin boards, and file sharing. Nearly all allow streaming video and audio. Most platforms allow instructors to monitor what each student reads, downloads, and watches (see Chapter 4). Typically, an organization will use a single learning management system (LMS) for all its courses. Loading software onto a network server is no harder than introducing other software. In corporate environments, firewalls may block unsecured Internet traffic from intruding into company systems; in that case, the software can be mounted on a local area network or intranet, or on a server that resides outside the firewall. Most instructors need help setting up courses. Accordingly, organizations engage instructional designers whose job lies somewhere between technical support and instruction (see Chapter 3).

No Significant Difference

Do students learn as well online as on-campus? Yes, according to the scholarly literature to date. In a widely cited report summarizing the results of such studies (http://nosignificantdifference.org/), Thomas L. Russell, director emeritus of instructional telecommunications at North Carolina State University, wrote, "The good news is that these 'no significant difference' studies provide substantial evidence that technology does not denigrate instruction." At Stevens, instructor Hosein Fallah tested that statement by teaching his course on US telecom-munications policy in conventional classes and on the Internet. To eliminate any bias, Fallah graded mid-term exams without knowing which of the classes they came from. As the literature predicted, the grades in both classes were practically the same (see Chapter 6). Naturally, not every student will find online learning to his or her liking. For one thing, it may require more discipline and maturity than conventional education. Nor do all instructors take to e-learning (see Chapter 5). A common criticism was articulated in the recent best-seller *The Social Life of Information* (Harvard Business School Press, 2000) by Xerox Corp. chief scientist John Seely Brown and University of California at Berkeley historian Paul Duguid. They argue that many schools are rushing to compete with for-profit companies by offering inexpensive "unplug and pay" courses. While online learning may add some value to an education, the authors contend, they cannot replace life on a real campus. Through the experience of attending class and meeting informally with peers and teachers, students gain more than mere information. They learn "distinct ways of judging what is interesting, valid, significant." Then, too, there are logistical questions raised by online learning. For the college professor, a chief concern is how much extra time will be consumed by producing and teaching a virtual course. Most academics feel their days are already full enough, what with classroom teaching, research, meetings, and other duties. For them, the most troubling thought may be that they will have to devote long hours responding to e-mail from students. Some online instructors find that the total time can far exceed a traditional course's classroom sessions and office hours. Loretta Donovan, former head of the distance learning program at Mercy College, Dobbs Ferry, NY, estimated that she devotes about 20 to 30 minutes per week per online student. Donovan once got 160 messages in 2 days from her students. "I'm very good at scanning," she remarked. That extra time is worth spending, Donovan said, because online courses offer a "much richer experience" than conventional classroom instruction. Not all instructors find online teaching more time-consuming. Hosein Fallah figures he works the same amount of time on his conventional and online classes, but the time "is distributed differently. Instead of being tied to a concentrated period of classroom teaching and office hours, you're online every day." Because Fallah also supplements his traditional courses with digital materials, he said, "I now get lots of e-mail from my in-class students, too." That trend is seen elsewhere in higher education. At Georgia Tech, for example, all on-campus undergraduate courses in electrical and computer engineering will include some digital learning components. Indeed, digital education's most profound effect is on campus, claimed Edward Borbely, Director, Center for Professional Development at the University of Washington. While engineering instruction has traditionally involved "writing on the board," with little interaction among students, he said, "Now professors are using websites as classroom tools." Because virtual instruction forces teachers to rethink their courses, many come away saying that their on-campus style has improved. To wean instructors from their dependency on classroom lecturing, Stevens introduced Web Faculty Colloquia, a program that gives those new to online instruction a chance to demonstrate their digital accomplishments and discuss their uneasiness about virtual pedagogy. New online teachers also receive intensive training in online software. So far, the results have been quite positive, with some previously reluctant professors emerging as enthusiasts.

Footing the Bill

While the introduction of online learning may not require breaking ground for new buildings, mounting a virtual education site is "certainly not free," observed Georgia Tech's Vice President for Distance Learning, Continuing Education and Outreach, "We're constantly scraping for funds to launch new programs." Faculty compensation is perhaps the biggest cost. At NYU's Tandon School, virtual faculty receive two fees, one for developing their digital course, another for teaching it. Additional administrative and technical staff is also needed, which, unlike traditional classrooms, must be kept up and running around the clock. Add the costs of faculty training, software licenses, e-commerce applications, Web design tools, upkeep of computer and telecommunications infrastructure, the bill for venturing into virtual space quickly balloons. Some institutions that have launched major online ventures, among them Pennsylvania State University's World Campus and the State University of New York's Learning Network, have spent many millions of dollars on infrastructure and staff (see Chapter 7). For the student, tuition for online courses is comparable to conventional classes.

Online Technical Course Catalog

Quite probably, certain types of instruction will never go entirely online, like laboratory courses that require access to expensive, specialized equipment. Nonetheless, since most industry labs are Internet enabled, it's likely that students will soon be linked online to nearly all up-to-date labs. A wide assortment of technical topics can be taught online. Stanford University was one of the first schools to provide digital instruction, and it now offers, through its Center for Professional Development, more than 250 technical and management courses to some 5,000 working professionals. Students can earn Master's degrees or take short courses in a number of engineering fields at many universities. NYU Tandon School of Engineering, which has introduced nine online graduate programs, known collectively as Tandon Online, teamed with IEEE, ACM, and other engineering professional societies that co-sponsor graduate courses aimed at "engineers in industry who need applications-oriented skill upgrades useful for their jobs and careers," explained Peter Wiesner, IEEE's former director of continuing education. Under the terms of the partnership, IEEE members receive 10 percent reduction in tuition. Some societies post online courses especially suited to their members' professional interests on web pages devoted to training and development. Others send routine e-mail messages and newsletters, alerting members to online technical courses offered by the society, universities, commercial vendors, and others designed to sharpen skills and concepts to enhance and update engineering practice.

Because of the way people live and work today, not to mention data showing that full-time, on-campus education occupies a much slimmer slice of the educational terrain, many colleges and universities believe that introducing alternatives to conventional teaching is a matter of their survival as educational institutions. Not that traditional classrooms will go away entirely. More likely, online learning will take its place alongside a range of options—an educational smorgasbord—from which the student will be able to pick exactly the right course at the right time and place.

This essay is an edited version of "Engineers Turn to e-Learning," published in IEEE Spectrum, *October 2000, pp. 59–63.*

INDEX